I
STILL
DO
DEVOTIONAL

I
STILL
D

DEVOTIONAL

31 Days to a Stronger Marriage

DAVE HARVEY

BakerBooks

a division of Baker Publishing Group
Grand Rapids, Michigan

© 2020 by Dave Harvey

Published by Baker Books
a division of Baker Publishing Group
PO Box 6287, Grand Rapids, MI 49516-6287
www.bakerbooks.com

Printed in the United States of America

Library of Congress Cataloging-in-Publication Data
Names: Harvey, David T. (David Thomas), 1960– author.
Title: I still do devotional : 31 days to a stronger marriage / Dave Harvey.
Description: Grand Rapids, Michigan : Baker Books, a division of Baker
    Publishing Group, 2020.
Identifiers: LCCN 2020003186 | ISBN 9780801094453 (hardcover)
Subjects: LCSH: Married people—Prayers and devotions. | Marriage—
    Prayers and devotions. | Marriage—Religious aspects—Christianity.
Classification: LCC BV4596.M3 H382 2020 | DDC 242/.644—dc23
LC record available at https://lccn.loc.gov/2020003186

Unless otherwise indicated, Scripture quotations are from The Holy Bible, English Standard Version® (ESV®), copyright © 2001 by Crossway, a publishing
ministry of Good News Publishers. Used by permission. All rights reserved.
ESV Text Edition: 2016

Scripture quotations labeled NIV are from the Holy Bible, New International
Version®. NIV®. Copyright © 1973, 1978, 1984, 2011 by Biblica, Inc.™ Used by
permission of Zondervan. All rights reserved worldwide.
www.zondervan.com. The "NIV" and "New International
Version" are trademarks registered in the United States
Patent and Trademark Office by Biblica, Inc.™

20   21   22   23   24   25   26   7   6   5   4   3   2   1

For Brent and Sally, because your marriage embodies the kind of stubborn grace that inspires us all to love steadfastly.

Contents

Sticking Together

Contents

Ending Together

Contents

How to Use This Devotional

Welcome to the *I Still Do Devotional*. I'm so glad that you've picked up this resource. Some of you may have grabbed this because you already know about the book *I Still Do: Growing Closer and Stronger through Life's Defining Moments* or the companion study guide. Some of you may know my previous book, *When Sinners Say "I Do."* Others have just found the devotional on its own. Whatever the case, I believe this book will serve you.

Over the years, Kimm and I have had some moments in our marriage when we just didn't know what to do. Those experiences often determined our progress and sometimes, quite honestly, have marked points where we plateaued. We learned that falling in love is easy; remaining in love is something entirely different. Kimm and I have often looked back and thought, *Gee, it would have been really nice to know that sooner!*

I've written this series of books to tell you about some of those defining moments. Think of defining moments as life-transforming experiences, events, and decisions that determine (and sometimes alter) your whole direction. We know that marriage is God-ordained, yet he seems to ordain specific defining moments *throughout* marriage. I'm talking about specific experiences or seasons in life where God

- presents a decision for truth
- requires a cost
- offers a Christ-exalting opportunity
- grows the soul
- determines our destination

In the book *I Still Do*, I chose ten crucial and defining moments, big life lessons that have shaped the direction of my marriage. But the truth is that most of those big moments were made up of smaller ones. The bigger lessons were learned bit by bit in the midst of what seemed like insignificant daily decisions. Sure, most of life is made up of ordinary days where big moments don't break into our monotony. We're not superheroes, spies, or sports stars who have one shining moment to rise above the routines of life. There are no gold medals for what most of us do. Our days are occupied with carpools, careers, and colon checks. Moments in our lives feel routine. Growth is about applying truth over time; it's a long, slow obedience. The truth is that God's invitations to us don't just come in the big moments of crisis. They come in the small moments of daily life. And without obedience in the little moments, we won't be ready to follow Christ when the big moments come. For that reason, we need daily reminders and daily reflection.

That's where this devotional comes in. This isn't the sort of book you should rush through. Go slowly with what's ahead. Read the daily Scripture passage and devotional alone or with your spouse. But even if you choose to read on your own, set aside some time to talk through the material with your spouse afterward. Each day includes a brief point of reflection, application, or prayer at the end that you can talk or pray about together. You may also consider writing down your and your spouse's reflections in a journal. Slowing down to write out these thoughts is a way of listening both to your spouse and to the Holy Spirit as he applies God's Word to your heart. My prayer is that through these thirty-one daily reflections, you'll see how Jesus wants to meet you in every moment of your marriage. He will make the difference for every decade.

STARTING TOGETHER

When You See God as Your Greatest Need

Ephesians 1:15–23

> I do not cease to give thanks for you, remembering you in my prayers, that the God of our Lord Jesus Christ, the Father of glory, may give you the Spirit of wisdom and of revelation in the knowledge of him.
>
> Ephesians 1:16–17

Meet Ron and Carla. Calling their marriage troubled does not begin to describe the poison that streams through their veins. Their evenings are filled

with skirmishes as they rehearse for each other, sometimes with palpable anger, the many ways their needs
remain unmet. Ron looks frantically for a time and
place where Carla will humbly surrender and acknowledge the supremacy of his need for respect. Carla needs
to feel loved in places that seem to be unreachable to
Ron. Their marriage has become a need-rumble, with
each spouse fighting over who wins the status of most
aggrieved.

Ron and Carla have been Christians for over a decade, and they attend a storied local church. But each
time the pastor teaches about marriage, Ron and Carla
walk away armed for another skirmish. The central
message they take away from each sermon or marriage
event is that husbands and wives have needs, and these
needs should be met. The unmet needs of husbands and
wives tends to be the central message.

What should they do? How can Ron and Carla stop
holding each other hostage and move forward together?

The concept of a need is porous and unruly. And married couples often use the term in a mixed-up way. The
tendency is for one spouse to see the other primarily as
a need-filler. By "need," I'm not thinking about true biological necessities like food, water, and shelter. Rather,

we tend to use the word "need" to refer to our exaggerated longings and the psychological deficits we feel. A husband, for instance, may act as if his wife was created for the sole purpose of making him happy—that is, for meeting his needs. When a man takes this posture, his "needs" very quickly become demands.

Conflict is sure to follow.

It's easy for experienced parents to see the problem when our teenage kids amp up the credibility of their desires by giving them some sort of biological urgency: "I need a girlfriend." "I need cologne." "If I don't get a pedicure, I think I'll just *die*!"

But here's the truth: none of these are really needs! The kids are exaggerating when they make their desires essential to survival. And we are too.

We kid ourselves when we think our spouse can meet all of our needs. It really doesn't matter whether we're talking about your true needs, your deepest longings, or your craven desires masquerading as legitimate needs—no human being can meet them all. You're not wired to find wholeness in or through a single individual other than Jesus. That person would need to be godlike (or be God), and that certainly doesn't describe you or the wonderful person you married.

What can help us think clearly about our unmet needs and desires? How does the Bible help us work through the conflict that inevitably comes when we cling to our expectations?

Much to our surprise, Scripture does not invite us to validate or satisfy every need we feel. We are invited to be a little self-suspicious. The Bible reminds us, "The heart is deceitful above all things, and desperately sick; who can understand it?" (Jer. 17:9). This means our hearts are capable of polishing any desire until it shines like a greedy beacon. I know this from experience. Sometimes my strongest felt need is for a bag of king-size Tootsie Rolls. But meeting that felt need would only sentence me to obesity and tooth decay and require that I do a lot of explaining to Kimm.

For marriages to last, needs must be examined in the light of God's Word.

God loves us infinitely, but he's not the cosmic need-fulfiller. On the contrary, God reveals himself in the Bible *as* our greatest need. This is not primarily because he is oriented toward us but rather because of God's eternal commitment to himself—to his own glory. God certainly loves us with an everlasting love (Jer. 31:3). But long before we were born, there was an enraptured and eternal affection between the Father, Son, and Holy Spirit. The timeless love shared eternally between the persons of the Trinity overflows in a desire to see the whole earth filled with God's glory (Hab. 2:14). The three persons within the Godhead delight in one another, and then God invites us to join the party. The Father of glory gives us his Spirit of wisdom and revelation simply so that we might know him (Eph. 1:17)!

What we need most for marriage is to be enthralled with God—with who he is and what he has accomplished through his Son, Jesus. When it comes to marriage—when it comes to all of life—knowing God is our greatest need.

And seeing God as our deepest need fundamentally changes the way we think about our marriage. The question is no longer "How can my spouse satisfy my needs?" but "How can my life and marriage bring glory to God?" The difference between those questions comes in the directions in which they pull us. Satisfying my need pulls me inward and makes my spouse a servant within my kingdom; my spouse exists to fulfill my desires. Seeing God as my greatest need pulls me outward toward his kingdom, where my marriage and my role as a husband or wife within it serves God's greater purposes.

When I see God as my greatest need, I'm free to move away from thinking about my own desires and expectations and toward thinking about my great responsibilities. And my greatest responsibility in marriage is love. Not the "Let's Get It On" *amore* that singer Marvin Gaye popularized, though I pray you enjoy plenty of that. I'm speaking of the eternal word spoken of in John 13:34, "A new commandment I give to you, that you love one another: just as I have loved you, you also are to love one another."

Marriage is a place where two sinners, mystified over the amazing mercy of God toward them, seek to outdo each other in giving preference, providing care, and displaying kindness. It's where each spouse points the other toward the daily grace available because of our Savior's sacrifice. Because God is our greatest need, helping our spouse see Jesus is the most substantial and ultimately satisfying thing we can do for each other.

Father of glory, help us to see that what we need most is to know and love you. Amen.

When You're Waiting for Change

Psalm 27; Titus 2:11–13

I believe that I shall look upon the goodness
of the LORD
in the land of the living!
Wait for the LORD;
be strong, and let your heart take courage;
wait for the LORD!

Psalm 27:13–14

Change is good. Our Christian life begins with re-generation, a complete change of heart. More-over, our walk with Jesus should be distinguished over time by change. The Christian life even concludes with a great finale of transformation when we are given glorified bodies and inhabit a new earth. It's not surprising that many of us feel that transformation in ourselves (and especially in our spouse!) should happen easily—with a simple touch of guidance, like a self-cleaning oven.

We all want immediate change. We want it to be as easy as walking into a dark room and throwing on a switch. Hear a passage, flip the switch of application, and change appears. That would make sense if Christianity were a vending machine: put in your coins and out pops your sanctification soda. But we all marry mere humans. Change in marriage is often slow. Very slow.

Your spouse may be inconsistent—saying one thing but doing another. Sometimes they move sideways, making little progress in areas where change is necessary. Sometimes they go backward, indulging outbreaks of annoyance, stubbornness, and resentment.

Or worse . . . they dig in and get rooted in downright frustrating places. Maybe your spouse has established an entrenched position that has stalled them spiritually and moved them away from God. Your heart breaks.

You love your spouse, but you are puzzled by their choices.

In these situations, it can be tempting to try to make things happen. It's not a self-righteous attitude necessarily. You just see how your spouse's decisions are stalling their growth, and you are wired for initiative. You're a fixer. You have ideas and suggestions. You want to help. There's this book, sermon, counselor, or biblical strategy that speaks especially to *this* situation.

So you talk. Talking about how your spouse needs to change makes you feel better initially, but it only makes them feel like a project. In reality, all of our talking can create the illusion of progress without any substantive movement. Pretty soon you're frustrated. You feel like nothing works.

When two people are yoked together, God's growth of one always has the other's soul in view. I think most of us understood this in theory when we got married. But no one told us that a long marriage can mean dealing with areas where our spouse doesn't—or won't—change, at least not according to our specifications or timetable. In truth, God orders the pace of our spouse's change—just as he orders our own process of transformation—in accordance with his own purposes. Sometimes he gives change slowly to humble us. This reminds us that we aren't divine; we aren't him. Sometimes he gives change slowly because that's what is necessary to tutor us in patience, love, and hope.

Sometimes we have no idea what God is doing. We don't have an iota of understanding about our circumstances or our spouse. But we wait for something more valuable than inside information. We wait to know Christ.

The gospel has appeared, and it teaches us to live upright and godly lives *while we wait* for Christ's appearing (Titus 2:11–15). This whole idea of waiting may feel counterintuitive. It's so docile, like you are running off the field to hit the showers and then take a seat in the stands. Why wait?

Waiting is about our heart's bent. When the gospel is at work in our heart, it has a chiropractic effect. It adjusts our soul away from self-sufficiency and shifts our posture toward God. We go from leaning away from God to leaning toward him, from being active in the flesh to active in the Spirit. Dependence replaces independence as our agenda for change in others is deleted and replaced with a quiet but dynamic trust in God's active warfare behind the lines on our behalf. Make no mistake. Waiting takes guts.

You see, in the Scriptures, waiting is never passive. In fact, it's an aggressive, faith-fueled activity. In this life, our growth in grace will always involve looking forward to that final, blessed hope. Waiting is a display of glorious weakness wherein we move deliberately and consistently toward God in prayerful dependence, asking him to do what only he can. David tells us that it takes strength and courage to wait (Ps. 27:14; 31:24). Far from being inert, waiting displays a deep and abiding faith in God's ability to respond. "But for you, O LORD, do I wait; it is you, O Lord my God, who will answer" (Ps. 38:15).

What kinds of changes are you waiting for? Bring them before the Lord right now and ask him for the strength and patience to wait.

When You Need to Know Your Heart

Proverbs 4:23; Luke 6:43–45;
James 4:1–6

Keep your heart with all vigilance,
   for from it flow the springs of life.

Proverbs 4:23

I n November 1863, Abraham Lincoln traveled by train to Gettysburg, Pennsylvania. Our sixteenth president had been asked to supply a speech to memorialize the casualties of the great battle of Gettysburg.

Ironically, President Lincoln was not even the main speaker. That honor fell to Edward Everett, a great orator and the president of Harvard University, who filled two hours with flourishes of eloquence that justified his reputation.

When Everett finished speaking, Lincoln stood to congratulate him and Everett took his seat. Nine thousand souls stood in a semicircle around the platform as Lincoln reached into his coat, pulled out a short sheet of paper, and delivered the Gettysburg Address. The entire speech lasted two minutes.

As Lincoln finished, the people stood motionless, stunned by the brevity and utterly transfixed by the words they had just heard. Lincoln assumed he had failed. History sees it differently. Edward Everett spoke for two hours and only a few historians remember he was there. Lincoln uttered 272 words, and children still memorize his speech to this day.

There are times when what is most needed to move people forward is short, simple, and straight to the heart. Proverbs 4:23 takes us to one of those moments. Married couples, whether newlyweds or beyond, must grasp essential truths from this verse in order to build a marriage that will endure.

First, *your heart directs your life.* In Scripture, our heart is presented as the center of our motivation. Our character, will, mind, emotions, inner life—all of these are captured within what the Bible calls the "heart." *It's who we really are!* Your heart is what sparks the anger you feel when your spouse offends you. Your heart is what draws your eyes to the wrong things online. Your heart is what makes you mad when you don't get your way with those you love. It's the window into why you do what you do.

It is a little disconcerting. We're accustomed to crafting our personality for the sake of public consumption. On social media, we can post, curate, and manage whatever persona or motivation we desire. But Proverbs 4:23 tells us that God looks below the surface of our Facebook profiles. He knows who we really are, because our hearts are always posted before him.

Husband and wife, do you know what drives you at the deepest level? Do you know what ultimately defines the direction you'll walk together? You may point to good things like your personal spiritual disciplines, exercise, jobs, friends, or family. You might think of bad things from your past—sin, demonic influence, or even crimes committed against you.

In Proverbs 4:23, God tells us what drives us. It's his version of the Gettysburg Address—short, simple, and valuable beyond measure. Of the heart he says, "from it flow the springs of life." Picture a water spigot turned on with no valve to stop it. The heart is always on; it always has desires and longings actively flowing from it. The heart is a manufacturing machine. In the same way that a clothing manufacturer produces shirts, pants, and suits, the human heart manufactures desires. And that factory never stops producing.

One specific way our heart directs our life is by moving our mouth. Our heart determines what we say. Jesus said, "The good person out of the good treasure of his heart produces good, and the evil person out of his evil treasure produces evil, for out of the abundance of the heart his mouth speaks" (Luke 6:45). If you are known for being kind and gracious to your spouse, it's probably because what's in your heart has found its way into your marriage through your speech. The opposite is true as well. "For out of the heart come evil thoughts, murder, adultery, sexual immorality, theft, false witness, slander. These are what defile a person" (Matt. 15:19–20). If you treat your spouse unjustly or live with a lack of love, it's simply a window into your inner world. Whatever fills the heart flows into the marriage.

Given that significant reality, it's easy to understand the second essential truth from this verse: *We must guard our heart with all vigilance!* By calling us to guard our heart, Scripture assumes it is vulnerable, delicate, fragile, and susceptible. It's easily disrupted. The Puritan author John Flavel once wrote, "Even a gracious heart is like a musical instrument, which, though it be ever so exactly tuned, a small matter places it out of tune again."[1] Tune a fine instrument, and it delights the ear. Bump it or allow it to sit unused, and it loses its tune. Our heart is the same. To have a marriage that lasts, we must attend to and tune our heart daily.

How well are you doing at tuning your heart to God and to each other? Do you pray together? Are you quick to encourage each other? What happens when you have conflict? Does anyone but the two of you know where you struggle, where you are vulnerable, where you could be taken down? When you feel stressed out, to what do you turn? Who are your friends, and why?

1. John Flavel, *A Saint Indeed, or the Great Work of a Christian in Keeping the Heart in the Several Conditions of Life*, Vintage Puritan Series (1826; repr., Louisville: GLH Publishing, 2015), ebook loc. 233–34.

Guarding our heart involves asking ourselves questions like these, and it also involves preaching the good news to ourselves. Here's the good news: Jesus became the perfect man. Though he wrestled with temptation (Luke 4:2; Heb. 4:15), his heart remained pure and undefiled. Thus, he was able to bear the penalty for all of the ways our heart is twisted and out of tune. Our heart may make our marriage vulnerable, but ponder this eternal truth: "God is greater than our heart" (1 John 3:20).

Jesus died in our place and rose on the third day. Then Jesus sent the Holy Spirit to convict our heart and purify our motivations. Now we have this promise: "Whoever believes in me, as the Scripture has said, 'Out of his heart will flow rivers of living water'" (John 7:38). Jesus changes our heart and fills it with new desires. That kind of living water makes for a great marriage.

Jesus, help us to trust you as the God who is greater than our heart. Amen.

When Your Family Lets You Down

Genesis 37:1–36; Romans 8:28

Do not be distressed or angry with yourselves because you sold me here, for God sent me before you to preserve life.

Genesis 45:5

Have you ever felt like your broken upbringing or your own personal history might destine your marriage to fail? There's no question that our upbringing exerts an enormous influence over us. It's tempting to think that your marriage is left to the fate of some combination of your genetics, the imprint of your parents' love or abandonment, the way they socialized you, and the way they modeled dealing with conflict. Particularly when your past is messy, it's hard to imagine a flourishing future.

But is our success really determined by the frailties and failures of our family history? To answer that question, let's survey the life of Joseph.

The drama of Genesis 37 introduces Joseph to us as a tattletale teenager, one who took great delight in bringing a bad report about his brothers to their father. That was right before things got really nasty. Joseph's family seemed to crave dysfunction like an addict craves opioids. Once Joseph threw his brothers under the bus, his vanity so eroded their relationship that his brothers "hated him and could not speak peacefully to him" (v. 4). Nevertheless, their father, Jacob, favored Joseph more than the others and gave him preferential treatment. This seemed to embolden Joseph, who then brazenly let his brothers in on his dreams of grandeur; dreams, by the way, that involved his brothers and parents bowing down to serve him.

You can guess the result: "They hated him even more for his dreams and for his words" (v. 8).

The tension grew to the point that the brothers decided to murder Joseph. But rather than have his blood on their hands, they settled on throwing him into a pit and selling him into slavery. For twenty shekels of silver, Joseph's eleven brothers abandoned him and trafficked him to Egypt. Then, to avoid getting caught, the brothers lied to their father, telling him that Joseph had been killed by a wild animal. And, in a staggering display of callous self-protection, they lived with the lie for years while their dad grieved the death of a son who they knew was actually alive.

How would you like to grow up under that roof?

Just consider the depth of this family's dysfunction. Jacob sent his favorite son to the brother-wolves, blindly unaware of the danger their bitterness posed. The brothers felt no family attachment or sense of protection toward Joseph. In fact, they conspired to kill him. Then, concluding that slavery was a more suitable—not to mention more lucrative—punishment, they victimized Joseph and betrayed their father.

If your family makes you wonder whether you can ever be normal, Joseph could probably relate. God designed the family to be a source of affirmation, support, development, and safety. For Joseph, it became the source of anguish and alienation. In a span of hours, Joseph went from favorite son to powerless slave. It was an enslavement that lasted for years. He was permanently displaced from his home. Because of the ways his brothers sinned against him, Joseph lived the rest of his life in a distant land.

And that's not even the full portion of Joseph's sufferings. Space doesn't allow for me to write about how Joseph was falsely accused, imprisoned, used, and forgotten. Joseph experienced a life where people's self-protection and self-obsession cost him dearly.

Yes, there were high points. In fact, Joseph eventually got married in Egypt. But if anyone had a right to enter married life feeling like damaged property, it was Joseph.

Can you identify? Maybe it happens when you're in conflict with your spouse; each time you toss an angry barb, you hear the voice of your father. Or perhaps your parents decided to divorce and you now wonder if you are predisposed to marital failure. Maybe you grew up in a home that was dysfunctional in ways you can barely describe, but that's the only model of family life you know.

Joseph would understand. He even made big mistakes that contributed to his issues. But that's not where Joseph's story ends.

You see, God determined the steps of Joseph's life. He moved miraculously to raise him from slavery to second in command over all Egypt. When a famine left Joseph's brothers starving in their homeland, they came to Egypt to find food. They never imagined that Joseph was still alive. They certainly didn't know about his prestigious promotion. When the brothers arrived in Egypt, the balance of family power shifted. Joseph controlled all of the supermarkets. The welfare of his family, those who had caused so much of his deep pain, was now in his hands.

But Joseph wasn't shackled to the past. His family's sins would not determine his response. In a moment of incredible drama, Joseph revealed himself before his brothers: "He wept aloud, so that the Egyptians heard it, and the household of Pharaoh heard it" (Gen. 45:2). Joseph's brothers were distressed, thinking it was payback time. But Joseph tenderly comforted them, saying, "Do not be distressed or angry with yourselves because you sold me here, for God sent me before you to preserve life" (45:5).

Joseph saw a purpose behind the family pain. He didn't deny the evil ("you sold me"), but he was now able to locate God in his family story ("God sent me"). God had a plan ("to preserve life") that included Joseph's pain. His family's dysfunction did not determine his future. In spite of his past, God blessed him.

At the center of the Christian faith lies the great injustice of the cross—the arrest, torture, abandonment, and crucifixion of the only sinless being ever to walk the earth. Yet that horrific injustice accomplished our salvation. That unjust act secured our relationship to God, our power to live a godly life, and the motivation to glorify God with our marriage. Next time you are worried about whether or not your family's brokenness will destroy your marriage, remember this truth: *Because of the pain of Christ's past, we now have a flourishing future.*

> *Father, we don't always understand your purposes in our past, but we trust that when people intend evil, your providential hand still guides. You are at work for our good. Amen.*

When You're Tempted

1 Corinthians 10:13; James 4:7–10;
1 Peter 5:8–9

No temptation has overtaken you that is not common to man. God is faithful, and he will not let you be tempted beyond your ability, but with the temptation he will also provide the way of escape, that you may be able to endure it.

1 Corinthians 10:13

There are a lot of temptations within a marriage. They come in all shapes and sizes. There are the common varieties—enticements toward anger, vanity, or self-righteousness. Money problems and difficult in-laws make us want to run away. One could think of all these as occupational hazards for marriage. Whether or not we say it out loud, most of us are aware of these temptations when we come to the altar. Our vows could rightly read, "I take you as my spouse . . . and accept these temptations along with you."

But more insidious than these real and relatable allurements are the more monotonous inclinations to simply neglect our spouse. If we're not careful, it's easy to have a marriage where busyness displaces affection. When kids come along, we can allow the roles of mom and dad to swallow up our identity as husband and wife. In these ways, the flesh, the world, and the enemy mount a coordinated assault upon our marriage.

Is it a real experience? Yes. Is it uncommon? No. First Corinthians 10:13 tells us, "No temptation has overtaken you that is not common to man."

Pause for a minute and let that sink in. Do you ever feel like your marriage has been singled out for a unique onslaught? Does it seem like Satan and several of his sadistic minions have dedicated themselves to spoiling your wonderful union? When Kimm and I first married, I suddenly felt less godly than when I was single. Granted, that was a self-assessment, but it made sense to me. It seemed like marriage made me sin, and I felt all alone in the battle. Satan can deceive us into thinking we're isolated when we're facing temptation. We believe scripts that sound something like this: "No one can relate to the fears we have about our future. No one can understand the rare facets of our complicated marriage. Few have walked the earth who can truly comprehend the pull I feel in the wrong direction. If each human heart is an archaeological dig, my temptations are unique and never-before-seen artifacts." We're a funny lot. We need to be seen as distinctive, special, and unique with any burden we bear.

The happy news is that the temptations you face are not unique. They're common to all people. And there's even more good news. It's not just other people who understand this fight. God is on your side as well. And there are potent promises for the struggles you're facing.

God is faithful. He *always* does what he says. God will keep every promise that he's made to you in the Scriptures. It's true! And consider the particular guarantee supplied in today's passage: "He will not let you be tempted beyond your ability, but with the temptation he will also provide the way of escape, that you may be able to endure it."

Stop reading for a moment and think about the greatest temptation facing your marriage right now.

Now consider God's promise. Jesus adores you. Your sovereign God, without being the author of evil, rules over the intensity of each temptation you face. He'll measure it perfectly to achieve his good purpose but not allow it to crush you. God created you. He knows your limits. He knows what should be allowed in your life. He knows what's needed to break you free from entrenched sinful patterns of doubt.

But God doesn't only tune temptation to our ability. He also provides a way out: "He will also provide the way of escape, that you may be able to endure it." If temptation is a burning house, you're not trapped inside. God meets you in the flames and springs you from the danger so that you can escape unharmed.

Go back to your marital temptation. If you are like me, you probably think a lot about the problem but little about the escape plan. Can you relate? If so, let me encourage you. Stop and take a fresh look at what's troubling or alluring you. Be honest about what your temptations are. God already knows them, and he stands poised to help you discover his faithfulness. Now think: Where is the escape hatch in this temptation that will bring you grace and help you to endure? Pray and ask God to help you see it.

Sometimes the way of escape is a simple act of subversion. Rather than spewing at your spouse, astound them with a surprising act of love. Maybe God wants to give you the gracious strength to flee what's enticing you. Maybe you simply need to shut off your phone each night when you come home. That's a strong romantic statement in the midst of a busy working world. God loves your marriage. He is faithful. There is a way of escape. Look around until you find it.

Father, meet me in this temptation. Help me to seek and find the way of escape that you provide. Amen.

When You Can't Trace
God's Intentions

Genesis 50:15–21; 2 Corinthians 1:8–11

Indeed, we felt that we had received the sentence
of death. But that was to make us rely not on
ourselves but on God who raises the dead.

2 Corinthians 1:9

The Puritans spoke of "the dark night of the
soul"—times when circumstances or sufferings confound us and we feel profoundly alone, often
even forsaken by God. The apostle Paul's experience
was much worse. It's one thing to feel weak. Maybe

you woke up that way this morning, depleted before your feet hit the floor. It's quite another thing to be "utterly burdened beyond our strength" (2 Cor. 1:8). Because you're married to a sinner, discouragement will sometimes body-slam your marital bliss. But it's another matter entirely to despair of life itself. We all hit pockets where the future feels hopeless, but that's a far cry from being under "the sentence of death" (1:9).

Has marriage ever crushed you? Have the walls of your dreams ever collapsed back in on you, making it impossible to see God from beneath the rubble? Maybe things detonated because the person you love betrayed you. Your marriage was supposed to last a lifetime, but it failed. Perhaps an unexpected illness stripped you of hope, or maybe one of your dear children went rogue and now wants nothing to do with either God or your family.

Are you in one of those moments where it's impossible to trace God's hand?

In 2 Corinthians 1, Paul writes about an experience that crushed him. He doesn't merely tell the story to elicit sympathy but to convey an essential truth about how God works in our disappointment and pain.

Paul had experienced affliction in Asia (vv. 8–9). We don't know the nature of his pain, but Paul describes it as "deadly peril" (v. 10). This affliction landed twin blows on Paul's soul. First, the unnamed affliction was beyond his strength to bear, and second, it caused him to despair of life itself.

Stop and reread verses 8–11. Slow down and peer at the wreckage Paul describes. Some unknown weight was crushing him. Something he had experienced felt beyond his strength to bear. Does that describe how you feel today?

The Greek word translated as "despair" in this passage implies the loss of a way of escape, the absence of any exit. Paul felt trapped (no way out), crushed (no strength), and in despair (no hope). He questioned his own survival.

Meanwhile, God's voice stayed silent, his will inaccessible. God seemed out of reach to Paul, like he was a million miles away. Is that where you or your spouse are right now? Do you feel trapped, crushed, alone, and hopeless? If you can relate to Paul's experience, God wants to meet you today. This is not simply a story about pain. Rather, Paul unveils for us a secret about how God will fill our pain with purpose.

Look carefully at the second half of verse 9: "But that was to make us rely not on ourselves but on God who raises the dead." Focus on those first few words: *But that was to make us*. The phrase implies an authority is at work enforcing a certain outcome. It's the mark left by an invisible hand. And what is the desperate situation making Paul do?

It boils down to three words. *Rely. Upon. God.*

You can't read this passage without the understanding that what we rely upon is serious business to God. But let's be uncomfortably honest for a moment. We don't take reliance as seriously as God does. Sure, we want a reliable car and a reliable job that carries reliable benefits. We certainly want to marry a reliable spouse. But this is an area where we're naturally bent toward a double standard. We value reliability in the people and things we depend on, but we're not nearly as serious about *being* reliable.

Yet God is so dead-set serious about developing reliability in us—and about cultivating our reliance upon him—that he uses some of our worst moments to achieve it. To be human is to be inconsistent. We pray grand prayers asking God to help us trust him. We don't expect God to answer our prayers by triggering afflictions, weakness, burdens, and despair. But Paul saw even the worst experiences as being designed by God for the believer's good. Sometimes God's best work for our growth and for the oneness of our marriage is done in the most remote parts of our soul, in the places where he seems most absent.

When Joseph fled from the seductions of Potiphar's wife, he passed a huge test of godly character. What did he receive in return? He was imprisoned for two years. There was no discussion, explanation, or even interpretation. God didn't send a prophet to sit with Joseph and patiently outline his intentions. We can understand what God was doing because we know how the story ends. But when you're in the story, with the daggers of uncertainty thrust through your soul, the affliction seems random, arbitrary, and meaningless. Yet God's hand was at work for Joseph, intending good and preserving life even when Joseph's brothers intended evil.

These reliance lessons are so important to God that he sometimes shakes our marriage without explaining why. But when we're forced to suspend judgment on his motives and actions, he sometimes shows us the deepest lessons. We serve One who is glorified more when he is trusted most.

So throw up your hands in surrender and choose to trust that God is at work for your good. In times like these, he will impale us on a cross and then call for a resurrection. And we, weak sinners that we are, will be reminded once again that God's invisible hand raises the dead.

Is your life or marriage being shaken by an invisible hand right now? Don't despair. God may not be seen, but he is at work, and part of his plan is to train you to rely upon him.

The Moment of Blame

Genesis 3:1–13

The man said, "The woman whom you gave to be
with me, she gave me fruit of the tree, and I ate."

Genesis 3:12

It's hard to admit when I'm wrong. It's hard to accept blame. In one of his *Calvin and Hobbes* comic strips, cartoonist Bill Watterson captures this perfectly.

Calvin remarks to his stuffed tiger friend, Hobbes, "I feel bad that I called Susie names and hurt her feelings. I'm sorry I did it." Hobbes answers, "Maybe you should apologize to her." Calvin thinks about this for a moment and replies, "I keep hoping there's a less obvious solution."[1] The way that Calvin's cogs are turning in this moment, it's no surprise in the next serial when his alter ego, Spaceman Spiff, arrives from the upper atmosphere with a welcome but all-too-obvious solution: "It's Susie's fault!"

In today's passage, Adam and Eve find that all-too-obvious answer quite quickly. Their story in Genesis 3 gives us a full tutorial on the character, nature, and tendencies of imperfect people. It doesn't just show us where sin *came from*, it reveals the devious way that sin *operates* within the human heart.

If Genesis were the *Star Wars* saga, chapter 3 would be like the stolen architectural plans of the Death Star. Except it is our plans that have been stolen. And they reveal specific ways we're vulnerable to attack and destruction. These plans show the particular places our enemies—the world, the flesh, and the devil—are most likely to attack.

Sin began with a deception: "Did God *really* say?" And after the man and woman gave in to it, the deception continued. One of the key ways we're deceived—one of

1. Bill Watterson, *Calvin and Hobbes*, Universal Press Syndicate, January 14, 1987.

the fundamental ways we remain weakened by original sin—is in our tendency to deflect blame, reject personal responsibility, and ascribe our sinful decisions to others. C. S. Lewis nailed it in observing, "Those who do not think about their own sins make up for it by thinking incessantly about the sins of others."[2]

This dynamic shows up almost immediately after the first wedding. Hurricane Satan hit the garden. The woman sought shelter in disobedience, and the man took cover in ambivalence. Both were wrong—dead wrong. But instead of owning it, Adam chose the all-too-obvious path: he tossed the woman under the bus.

Part of original sin's fiber—part of its character—is the tendency to deflect agency and ascribe our sinful decisions to others. When he blames the woman, Adam shifts his God-ascribed moral responsibility away from himself and tags her: "The woman whom you gave to be with me, *she* gave me fruit of the tree" (Gen. 3:12, emphasis mine). This seemingly clever evasion on the man's part reveals a potent desire embedded in all sin. Sin seeks to shift our status before God and others from being morally responsible (and therefore culpable) to

2. C. S. Lewis, *God in the Dock* (Grand Rapids: Eerdmans, 2014), 127.

being the victim of other people's decisions. The ultimate insanity is that we convince ourselves we are also victims of God's decisions. After all, "the woman whom *you* gave to be with me" delivered the fruit.

When sin arrives for work, it clocks in early and puts in overtime. When sin speaks, it supplies our hearts with a passive voice. "Me?" says Adam. "I'm just a bundle of goodness enjoying the garden—walking and talking with God, spreading his glory. The bad things are happening *to* me. It's *that* woman, Lord. *She* gave it to me!" In Adam's mind, sin was done to him, not by him. Moral agency was swapped for self-pardon. Under the sway of sin, his self-understanding had only one category—sinned *against*.

When sin knocks, everyone is guilty except me. Even God!

What about you? Have you ever noticed that when you tell your story, including some of your trials and pains, you're rarely positioned in the story as a sinner with all your junk? More often we see others on the stage as actors, committing sins against us or omitting things they should have done for us.

The problem is that when we lose our sinfulness, we obliterate our need for a Savior. For our psychological issues, we may need a therapist. For our ulcer, we need a doctor. For our root canal, we need a dentist. But if we are basically good, we only need roles that will help elevate our consciousness or good works to the place of perfection. Only sinners need a Savior. Only those who are hopelessly lost need God to clothe himself in flesh and come after them. Acknowledging our sin is actually the first step in our journey of needing and knowing the Savior.

What steps could you take to better see and own your sin? Pray over what you see. Then thank God for his eternal and sacrificial love, demonstrated when he sent his Son to rescue you from your sins!

The Moment of Humility

Philippians 2:1–11

Do nothing from selfish ambition or conceit, but in humility count others more significant than yourselves.

Philippians 2:3

Joey loved his wife and family. He just loved his job more. Life at home seemed to plod along, confining him to a monotonous path. His job, however, was a mountain with many trails to the top. Just thinking about his work stoked his endorphins. Joey could feel an adrenaline rush as he drove up to the building. And his job had incentives! Money, prestige, and advancement came quickly, a clear confirmation that the work was God's will. After all, Joey's success was an opportunity to let his light shine before others (Matt. 5:16). Joey was confident that his industrious, single-minded dedication made him a better witness. Surely his work ethic—not to mention his talent—would make others want to be like him.

That was Joey's perspective. In reality, Joey lived in a delusional world, one where he spiritualized his self-ish ambition. He saw long obedience in the routines of home life as poor stewardship. He thought God treasured his self-consuming conceit. The truth is that Joey was sacrificing his marriage, children, and spiritual health on the altar of his ambition. To map Philippians 2:3 onto Joey's life, you'd need to revise it to read, "Do what you can from selfish ambition or vain conceit, and in that confidence consider yourself more significant than others." Joey thought of himself as a shining witness, but he was more like a black hole.

Joey's tale is all too familiar. That's why the lesson I want you to learn may sound pretty crazy. Ready?

Marriage requires ambition—lots of it.

If that statement unsettles you, this may be due to your definition of ambition. When I write statements like that, some Christians understand me to say that marriage requires an amoral, me-centered, power-hungry, self-warping orientation. They think of all ambition as despoiled desire—rotten fruit from a poisonous tree.

But if you look closely, Paul does not forbid all ambition in this passage. The apostle has corrupted aspirations—what he calls "selfish ambition"—in his crosshairs. When our drive for glory is turned inward and, like Joey, we set ourselves in the middle of our dreams, we're in danger. Many marital unions have been shattered by the inexorable pursuit of position or influence, envy over a spouse's opportunities, or entitled prioritizing of *my gifts* or *my hobbies*. Such selfishness is like a spreading disease that infects everything in its wake.

When the world revolves around *me*, the world is way too small. In my quest to be great, I shrink. It's with good reason that Paul says to "do nothing" from this motivation.

But godly ambition, the kind marriage really requires, is different. It's a God-implanted desire to see God use your life and marriage for *his* glory. When couples unite their godly ambitions in a marriage, good stuff happens. Love grows. Businesses launch. Churches are planted. Families start. The poor are resourced. Good works are empowered. The list is endless! And here's the thing. It doesn't happen at the expense of marriage. In fact, it more often happens through the synergy of marriage.

Husbands and wives, are you caught in the web of selfish ambition? If so, a marriage filled with godly ambition, one with creative synergy working together for your good and God's glory, is possible. Don't miss this beautifully simple next step. Paul writes, "In humility count others more significant than yourselves." God wants you to start with a different kind of accounting. He wants you to begin adding up what is valuable in your life in a new way. Specifically, he wants you to count your spouse as more significant than yourself. If you're wondering what that looks like, here are some questions to kick-start your thinking.

1. **How often do you encourage your spouse?** You can't affirm good things in your mate if you don't stop long enough to count up their good qualities. One of the reasons God calls us to "encourage one another and build one another

up" (1 Thess. 5:11) is that it breaks us free of our obsessive self-interest. After all, it's hard to be conceited when you're celebrating the value of others.

2. **How often do you ask your spouse for help?**
One way to count your spouse as more significant is to consider their opinion as more important than your own. Few things make a spouse feel more secure than when they know their opinions are valued by the one they love. Go to your spouse for counsel. You may be surprised by the way God blesses that step of humility.

3. **How often do you consider the claims that the Savior's example makes upon your marriage?**
Philippians 2 wasn't merely designed to give you some practical handles. The arc of this chapter moves toward the self-emptying act of Christ's incarnation. When God calls us to humility, he's not merely calling us to virtue but also to discipleship—to follow the One "who, though he was in the form of God, did not count equality with God a thing to be grasped, but emptied himself, by taking the form of a servant,

being born in the likeness of men" (Phil. 2:6–7). Christ's humility as revealed in his life, death, and resurrection is a portrait of self-emptying love, and that's the true motivation and power behind counting your spouse as more significant than yourself.

Maybe today it's time to get a new ambition, one that displaces you from the center and turns you toward your spouse with a sincere desire to truly make them the *significant* other.

Father, give me a new ambition to count my spouse as more significant than myself and to count Jesus as the greatest treasure of all.

The Moment of Marital Need

Hebrews 4:14–5:10

For we do not have a high priest who is unable to sympathize with our weaknesses, but one who in every respect has been tempted as we are, yet without sin.

Hebrews 4:15

A couple of years back, I preached at our Good Friday service. During the message, I made a passing reference to a passage from Hebrews that resonated deeply with our church folk. It was one of those unforeseen moments when a Bible verse pierces the chaos of crazy-busy lives, tapping the brakes so we could slow down and listen. You may find that it tolls a bell of hope for what you need in your marriage right now. That verse was Hebrews 4:15, where the author describes Jesus Christ as our high priest, who relocated from heaven to become the sacrifice and mediator for his people. In this verse we learn that when Jesus takes the role of high priest, he endows it with an unusual quality: sympathy with our weakness.

Don't rush past this point. This verse invites us to ponder an elusive truth about ourselves that can be hard to see and difficult to admit. Here it is: *Jesus assumes we are weak.*

This verse addresses every couple who has walked the aisle and whispered "I do" with Jesus in view. We're all fragile sojourners in a fallen world. We're frail, tenuous, and imperfect. All of us. This verse isn't addressing some subset of people who have the unique misfortune of being flawed. If you breathe, you are weak. It's not a question of whether or not it's true; it's a question of whether or not you're clued in.

Recently I left my cell phone out in the rain. It's the third time this has happened in recent memory. Kimm is really patient when I misplace something, but I drive myself nuts over it. I feel like I should just take my new cell phones and pitch them in the lake. With each incident, it feels like a prophet has arrived to announce the decline of my once-organized mind. I am weak, and every day there are more clues.

Life reminds us of our weakness. It shows us that we're not angels impervious to going gray or New Age gurus who sense our minds and bodies growing stronger each decade. Not even close! We're the fabulously fallen and frail ones who lose our keys, forget appointments, say stupid things, and, yes, even get speeding tickets. (Oh, I know . . . you were innocent.) We are not omniscient, omnipotent, or omnicompetent. We are weak.

And in case you're wondering, it's not all about sin. Sure, all sin reveals weakness, but not all weakness is sin.

For married folks who own this truth, this passage offers a mind-blowing message: *Jesus gets us*. Jesus is not detached from the real frustrations we encounter. He's no Pharisee, outwardly tolerating us but inwardly reviling our weakness and rolling his eyes when we fail. No, Jesus actually sympathizes with us where we are weak. As our loving High Priest, he empathizes with the areas where we suffer defects and deficiencies.

That's not all. Jesus doesn't sympathize as a stranger who's struggling to relate. He's not the guy who once watched a video on weakness or someone who quickly consulted an expert to become conversant. No, the Savior knows weakness on the level of experience. As our perfect High Priest, Jesus is the "one who in every respect has been tempted as we are" (Heb. 4:15).

Husband or wife, just think about that. In *every* respect he was tempted as we are. Did you have some anger eruptions with the kids this week? Jesus understands. He's felt that temptation. Are you struggling with an insensitive comment your spouse made? Jesus gets it. He was mocked, slandered, and scandalized; he knows that pain. Are you afraid of the future? Not sure you can make it? Jesus understands; he sweat blood in Gethsemane and prayed that God might spare him. Jesus understands the battle because he's been to war. He gets you.

And here's one last bit of good news to encourage your soul. Because Christ is able to sympathize with our weakness, we don't need to pity ourselves. If you're like me, any time that I become aware of another weakness, it's like I've received a decorated invitation to an immediate pity party. Most days you're invited too. "Come join Dave as he spends yet another day sulking over the fact that he's not God!"

Thankfully, God speaks a better word. "Hey, Dave," Christ says, "let's turn the self-pity dial down a bit. Remember, I'm the perfect High Priest. Sympathizing with you is *my* job. I've got it covered. Why don't you just think about how to love and enjoy your wife today!"

The good news of how Christ loves me when I'm weak breaks through my self-pitying tendencies. I'm reminded that through Christ's death and resurrection, I get far more sympathy than I deserve. At the cross I not only avoid getting the just judgment my sins rightfully warranted, but in place of God's wrath I receive his adoption, his loving affection, and his compassion for my weakness. Instead of the antipathy I earned, I get sympathy as a child of my heavenly Father.

Are you feeling weak and smacked around by temptations today? Have you just printed invites to your own pity party? The good news of the gospel includes a great High Priest, a Savior with a love so vast that he drops into the moments of our weakness and temptation and says, "I get you. I understand."

Do you spend more time looking for pity for yourself or receiving the sympathy Christ already has for you?

The Moment of Weakness

2 Corinthians 12:1–21

But he said to me, "My grace is sufficient for
you, for my power is made perfect in weakness."
Therefore I will boast all the more gladly about my
weaknesses, so that Christ's power may rest on me.

2 Corinthians 12:9 NIV

Kimm and I moved through our first decade not
really understanding how God's strength is
found in weakness. We definitely had thorns in those
first ten years. The unexpected kind. For instance, marriage and parenting exposed me. To be a good husband
and then a decent dad, I needed God in ways I'd never

imagined—way more than I thought. It's funny. I think I sailed through my twenties and thirties (and even into my forties) expecting that the cumulative wisdom gained from those years would diminish my experience of weaknesses. In reality, I gained a more accurate accounting of my weaknesses. When our kids became teenagers, jobs became more demanding, bills escalated, and family activity hit overdrive. Our natural strength declined, our temptations sharpened, and our bodies aged. We knew weakness. We became more desperate for Christ, and because of that, hopefully we became more mature.

But even as I learned to acknowledge my inability, I still had more to learn. At that point, I didn't yet see our weaknesses as gifts given to us by Jesus to accomplish something eternal. Part of me hoped that my sense of weakness would diminish as my marriage grew older. And sure, knowing each other better and sharing love and pain provided a strong foundation to build many memories and weather some big storms.

But then something bigger happened. As we moved into our second and third decade together, I began to see that the weaknesses imposed and exposed by marriage were part of God's design. When I write that,

I'm not blaming God for all the areas where I fail. I'm just saying God is an expert at taking experiences that elate us—experiences like marriage and parenting—and using them to school us in dependence and trust.

Over time I have come to see God's purpose in the thorns more clearly. God values our trust and dependence on him more than our perfected behavior, more than our strength. He did not give me marriage to display my power or even to make me stronger, but rather to reveal his strength and power through my weaknesses.

The first step on this path toward grace is deepening dependence. God wanted to use our marriage as a place where I could learn to rely on him. He designed it to be a place where every reassertion of my independence from him would be met with a resounding reminder that I am desperate. In that weakness, he has shown me again and again that I need Jesus.

Thorns deepen our dependency. Paul Barnett writes that the apostle Paul's thorn "kept him from imagining himself as a spiritual superman. The 'thorn' also kept Paul pinned close to the Lord, in trust and confidence."[1]

1. Paul Barnett, *The Message of 2 Corinthians*, The Bible Speaks Today (Downers Grove, IL: InterVarsity, 1988), 178.

Think about your life right now. Think about your marriage. What are the areas that pin you close to the Lord? Some confounding area of your spouse's behavior? A physical affliction? Your family finances? A prodigal child? Thorns can be deceptive because they're often small. But when they pierce our flesh, small thorns can feel like giant nails.

If you're wondering why something as wonderful as marriage can remain hard through different seasons, you might think about how God delivered a thorn to Paul after his magnificent experience in the third heaven. Sometimes good experiences deliver us to tempting places. Our heart exalts in the experience of the good rather than the Giver of the good. So, in an act of love, God will at times take the things we might be tempted to exalt over and convert them into a desperate need for him.

The second step along the path is an experience of his power in our weakness. I'm so thankful that the good news of the gospel includes a great High Priest, a Savior with a love so vast that he drops into the mundane moments of my weakness and temptation, looks straight at me and my spouse, and says, "I get you, and I understand."

That's goodness and grace from the God who gets us! He is the *perfect* High Priest for weak people like you and me (Heb. 9:11–12). When thorns are pressing deep, the gospel comes to us with amazing news. It tells us that the thorns are not God's punishment for our sin. This good news helps us wake up each morning aware that our greatest problem has been solved. The wrath we deserved was resolved when it was released upon Jesus Christ.

But there's something else. In the place of that wrath, we get forgiveness from sin, reconciliation to God, adoption into his family, and a permanent home with Jesus when we die. Do you see how this might change how we think about our weaknesses and thorns? We can live satisfied today, not because we have all we desire but because we have received more than we deserve. I love this quote from Barbara Duguid, which gets at the heart of both these truths:

> The mature Christian is much stronger than he was before because he has a deeper and more constant sense of his own weakness. God has been teaching him this lesson for a long time, and by the loving grace of his heavenly Father, his suffering has not been in vain!

His heart has deceived him so many times that he has learned to distrust himself more readily and make provision for his own weakness. Because the grown-up Christian knows that he falls easily, he avoids situations that are difficult and tempt him to sin. He is wary of Satan's tricks and asks for help quickly from other Christians and from God. He is not too proud to admit his failures, confessing and repenting rapidly when he falls. He is also not so easily disappointed in himself and others because his expectations have changed and he now understands that both he and his fellow believers are very weak and can do nothing without Christ, for he has learned to run to the throne of grace quickly in his times of need. As the Lord told the apostle Paul, "My grace is sufficient for you, for my power is made perfect in weakness" (2 Corinthians 12:9). He is stronger in Christ and not in himself.[2]

Father, thank you for good news that provides power in the moments of my weakness. Amen.

2. Barbara R. Duguid, *Extravagant Grace: God's Glory Displayed in Our Weakness* (Phillipsburg, NJ: P&R, 2013), 63.

STICKING TOGETHER

DAY

11

The Moment of Mystery

Ephesians 5:21–33

"Therefore a man shall leave his father and mother and hold fast to his wife, and the two shall become one flesh." This mystery is profound, and I am saying that it refers to Christ and the church.

Ephesians 5:31–32

Marriage brings mystery. I'm not talking about the inexplicable allure between men and women or the enigma of all those guys who marry way out of their league. ("How did he get HER?!") No, the mystery here is that Christian marriages speak. They're designed to say something. The question is, what statement is your marriage making?

In Ephesians 5, Paul takes his readers back to the first wedding in the garden of Eden. We're familiar with it. The man and the woman were introduced, got married, and then immediately tumbled into the horror of temptation and sin. The first marriage remained intact, but everything else was broken. But when Paul writes about the first marriage, he stops the story at the end of Genesis 2—before the fall. He does so in order to give us the hidden backstory for this first union. Paul tells us that God embedded something profoundly mysterious in the institution of marriage. He designed it to point to a greater reality. God designed "I do" to be a picture of Christ and his love for the church.

I remember reading a story about a person who fell in love with an inexpensive painting and immediately purchased it. When they got it home, they discovered a second painting—a priceless classic from one of the old masters—hidden beneath the canvas. They purchased the original because they loved it, only to discover that it was more valuable than they could have dared to dream.

Most Christians approach marriage functionally, like a business partnership in which a couple collaborates to feed the kids, pay the bills, and enjoy permissible sex. We can spend our lives being friends and companions and still fail to realize that our marriage, like that painting, carries with it another purpose, one with indescribable worth. John Piper explains it this way:

> The mystery is this: God did not create the union of Christ and the church after the pattern of human marriage—just the reverse! He created human marriage on the pattern of Christ's relationship to the church.
>
> The mystery of Genesis 2:24 is that the marriage it describes is a parable or symbol of Christ's relation to his people. . . . When God engaged to create man and woman and to ordain the union of marriage, he didn't roll the dice or draw straws or flip a coin as to how they might be related to each other. He patterned marriage very purposefully after the relationship between his Son and the church, which he had planned from all eternity.[1]

When husbands and wives exchange vows, our marriages aren't merely about us. The Bible tells us that our

1. John Piper, *Desiring God: Meditations of a Christian Hedonist* (Colorado Springs: Multnomah, 2011), 213.

marriages speak. They make statements about Christ's love for his church. If someone spent the evening in your house observing your marriage, what statement would they hear?

Recently Kimm and I had a conflict where I was dismissive of her. In retrospect, it was quite a display of arrogance. I stepped right on top of her perspective and confidently asserted my take on things. Fortunately God convicted me, and I was able to confess my sin. But when I behave in those ways, I'm not making a clear statement about Christ's love for the church. I'm making a loud statement about my love for myself.

As you think about your marriage today, what statement is it making about Christ? If the statement is not what it should be, don't immediately despair. Regardless of where your marriage is today, the gospel can change what your marriage says. Remember your Savior! Because of the cross and resurrection, your poor example, along with the guilt and condemnation it incurs, is not the final statement over you. God has made a louder statement—a statement that is utterly intractable. God loves you with an everlasting love. He has forgiven your sins, adopted you into his family, and given you the Holy Spirit, who supplies you with the grace and power to change.

> *Father, help our marriage to be more than functional. Empower us in love so that our marriage is the clearest gospel message that we preach. Amen.*

When Your Marriage Needs the Church

1 Timothy 3:4–15; Hebrews 10:24–25

> And let us consider how to stir up one another to love and good works, not neglecting to meet together, as is the habit of some, but encouraging one another, and all the more as you see the Day drawing near.
>
> Hebrews 10:24–25

You may not know the name Esther Pauline Lederer, but you likely know her pen name, Ann Landers. Landers was a wildly popular human interest and advice columnist until her death in 2002. If you followed her, you know that some of the stories she shared were doozies:

Dear Ann Landers,

On a train to Germany, I was seated next to a friendly looking, middle-aged lady. She appeared to be an American, so I asked if she was from the United States. She gave me an icy stare and immediately started to read a book—in English. (The train had not yet left the station.)

A few moments later, the conductor came along to collect tickets. He glanced at this woman's ticket and excitedly began to rattle off something in German. She ignored him. A gentleman across the aisle shouted at her, "Did you understand what he said?" More silence. He repeated the question. She paid no attention. Once again, he repeated the question.

Finally, the loner replied crisply, "NO! And I don't care to have any conversations with YOU either."

The traveler shot back, "Too bad, because the conductor was trying to tell you you're on the wrong train, going in the wrong direction, and this is an express that doesn't make a stop for six hours."

By that time the train had pulled out and we were on our way.[1]

When I first read this story, I found it oddly encouraging. It reminded me that I'm not the only one who does really dumb things when I'm traveling. But there's a bigger point to be drawn from this story—one that goes right to the heart of a lasting marriage. *We need help on our journey.*

Sure, you could attempt to go it alone. Many couples do. But they often find themselves making progress in the wrong direction. Churches may seem to have an endless supply of meetings, but the writer of Hebrews tells us their goal: "to stir up one another to love and good works." Journeys can be tricky and sinners can be senseless. We need to be stirred up to keep loving our spouse. We need to be inspired to do good works at home. We need to encourage others and be encouraged by others in order to go the distance. According

---

1. "Ann Landers," *Delta Democrat Times*, August 24, 1975. Accessed online at https://newspaperarchive.com/delta-democrat-times-aug-24-1975-p-28/.

to the writer of Hebrews, if we're going to finish the race, then we need our local church.

My heart breaks for Christian couples who go it alone. They hit hard times with no one to encourage them. They get locked in marital conflict with no one to pray for them or offer a helpful perspective. I've lost count of the number of times that I've sat with my pastor to gain perspective on the future—and that's just this year! Married couples need to learn a lesson from the stubborn tourist above. We need other travelers to keep our marriage on the right track.

Where do you rate the importance of the local church for your marital health? Is it an optional extra on the journey—like a skeet shooting excursion on a Caribbean cruise? Here's how Paul describes the local church: it's the "household of God . . . a pillar and buttress of the truth" (1 Tim. 3:15). God ordained the church to be the people who hold one another up with the Word. It's where we help each other learn to apply the truth. Commands like those in Ephesians for a husband to "love his wife as himself" and for a wife to "see that she respects her husband" (Eph. 5:33) can be abstract and esoteric. But in the local church, application is embodied. You see the truths lived out in the lives of other married couples. Older and wiser men can disciple and train a younger man to love his wife, and a wife can observe how older and wiser women model respect for their husbands. The local church becomes the venue where we unite with other like-minded married people to learn how to please God on the journey.

Yes, it's possible to travel alone and unbothered and still survive the journey. But that trip is a dangerous journey. God designed us so that our endurance in life and marriage is dependent on him and vitally connected to others. Take stock of your life today. Don't be a stubborn tourist, speaking to no one while you travel in the wrong direction. Consider right now what steps you can take to move toward a local church.

Is the local church part of your strategy for a lasting marriage? Is your marriage benefiting from the prayer, encouragement, counsel, and challenge that can only come from joining in relationship with other believers?

When You Carry
Someone's Shame

Hebrews 12:1–3

Looking to Jesus, the founder and perfecter of
our faith, who for the joy that was set before
him endured the cross, despising the shame, and
is seated at the right hand of the throne of God.

Hebrews 12:2

Today we look at a delicate topic—the soul-
stabbing pain of loving a prodigal. Maybe it's
a spouse living in rebellion or a child revolting against
your parenting. Maybe it's a sibling trapped in a hidden

addiction. Bottom line is, you love someone who is going rogue.

Whether you are the spouse, parent, or relative of a prodigal, these relationships often have a common denominator: *As Christians, we bear a unique burden of shame.* It sounds counterintuitive, doesn't it? We believe Christ *bore* our shame (Heb. 12:2). The gospel *unshackles* us from sinful disgrace (Rom. 5:5), and "everyone who believes in [Christ] will not be put to shame" (Rom. 10:11). So why does loving a prodigal come with such heavy shame?

The problem isn't God. It's his people.

We know the church is uniquely qualified to help sufferers. Just look at our assets—the gospel, community, prayer. But when a spouse or parent bleeds for their wayward loved one, the church can be quick to judge and slow to bind wounds. We can dish out shame rather than demolish it. As a result, Christians gravitate elsewhere for help, intuitively sensing their church is not a place of grace.

If you are living in that place right now or you are close to someone else experiencing it, what can you do that will make a difference today? Here are four thoughts.

First, face your fear. Katy was raised in a Christian home, attended a Christian school, went to youth group, and recorded a gospel album as a teenager. When she sang, people wept. But Katy had other desires. She left home for Hollywood and recorded a racy hit in 2008 titled "I Kissed a Girl." You guessed it. I'm writing about superstar Katy Perry. Mary Hudson, Katy's mom, recently said, "I get a lot of negative vibes. People ask, 'How could you have a daughter like that?'"

That question betrays a haunting fear embedded within the church: "Could I have a child or a spouse like that?" Rebellious churchgoers trigger serious anxieties for Christians. We play the comparison game, examining prodigals and their loved ones to find differences between *us* and *them*, *our* kids and *their* kids. To assuage our own worry, we want to find something to explain, something to blame. But comparison creates a callous culture where suspicion trumps compassion, speculation replaces intercession, and judgment supplants long-suffering. All Christians are called to suffer. For some, the pain comes through a prodigal. We must normalize this if the church truly is going to be a place of grace.

Second, look for or offer safe space. Do you love a wayward soul? If so, I pray you enjoy a safe space, one with open ears, wide hearts, and unhurried conversation. One where friends bear grief, withhold judgment, protect confidentiality, and meet shame with gospel hope. Safe space doesn't mean unaccountable, godless venting or assuming every wayward sufferer is a victim. But most parents or spouses of wanderers come to church believing, at least on some level, that they're at fault. And that floating blame distracts them from real hope.

When you hear the words *wayward* or *rebellious* tumble from a parent's lips, hear *grief*. Grieve with them (Rom. 12:15). Don't be a fixer! Entrust any discovery of culpability to God and time. It's not the immediate priority. The more we comprehend grace, the more we stop identifying their sin and start sympathizing with their suffering.

Third, label the legalism. One of the less-detected strains of legalism in the church today is the false hope of deterministic family life. This unspoken but deeply felt dogma assumes that one spouse's faithfulness determines the spiritual health of the marriage. It's the same with raising kids: "If I obey the Bible, discipline consistently, and push the catechism, then my children will look good on earth and be present in heaven." No one would claim it, but it's justification by parenting. Such legalism smuggles in a confidence that God rewards faithful moms and dads with obedient, converted kids and does so proportionally to what they deserve.

We also flip it. If the gospel of determinism is true, a wayward spouse reveals personal failure. When a marriage spins out of control, one or both spouses are just reaping what they've sown. I'm not suggesting that our obedience doesn't matter. Godly parents, for instance, influence children positively, and bad parenting influences them negatively. But the key word is *influence*. Too many Christians unconsciously confuse influence with determinative power. This assumption takes God, the world's brokenness, and the human will out of the equation. Remember, God is the perfect Father, and he still has prodigal children (Luke 15:11–32; Rom. 3:12).

Fourth, celebrate the Shame-Bearer. When the spouse or parents of a prodigal attend a church event, shame tags along. This invisible companion whispers within about how substandard they are compared to the other gold-circle group that gathered. Seeing happy families can prompt pangs of guilt, convincing them that no one could relate to their circus at home. Shame baits them to focus *inward* on their flaws or *outward* on their circumstances. One of my daughters used to run with her head down, never looking where she went. After a few bumps and bruises, she learned a valuable lesson: the best way to move forward is to look up.

To suffocate shame, we must help hurting spouses and parents look up to Jesus, "who for the joy that was set before him endured the cross, despising the shame" (Heb. 12:2). The words "endured the cross" transport us back to the most dishonorable hours in human history. Jesus had friends but none stuck by him. One betrayed him. Another denied him. His followers? One week they sang "Hosanna!" and the next cried "Crucify!" He was entirely innocent yet was scorned as the worst of sinners. Jesus knew deep shame, but the surprising twist comes in his response. *He despised it*. Christ despised shame because he saw beyond it. Shame is painful, but it was powerless to define Christ. Shame could not change his identity or control his future. Jesus saw joy beyond it. Christ nailed our shame to the cross. In its place, he imputed to us his record of perfect righteousness. When God looks at us, he doesn't see our marriage or parenting failures. He doesn't scroll through an unfiltered feed of ugly accusations and regrets. God sees his Son instead of us. We must look to Christ as well. For anyone who loves a wayward soul, shifting one's gaze is the only link to present sanity and future hope.

How can you help your church become a place of grace for those with tender wounds? How can you face your fear, offer safe space, label the legalism, and celebrate the Shame-Bearer?

The Moment of Comfort

2 Corinthians 1:3–7

Blessed be the God and Father of our Lord Jesus Christ, the Father of mercies and God of all comfort, who comforts us in all our affliction, so that we may be able to comfort those who are in any affliction, with the comfort with which we ourselves are comforted by God.

2 Corinthians 1:3–4

How does God create a person who is skilled in comforting their spouse? Is it simply a matter of DNA and disposition? You've met those genetically sweet souls who were born to care, who are predisposed to sympathize and hardwired to ask questions, and who ooze concern. They're the burden-bearers who thrive on your chaos. But you look in the mirror and you know that person—or frankly anything close to that person—is not staring back at you.

Here is the truth. We're all bent inward toward self-care, self-concern, and self-comfort. Our spouse's pain is an unwelcome distraction from our extended self sessions. We look up and wonder who dares to divert us from our comfort expedition. So how does God take people fixed on self-comfort and turn them outward toward others? How does he move our narcissistic gaze away from our own reflection and make us look up at the pain around us? How does God take people who aren't inclined to care and transform them into comforters?

Recently, Zeke got hit with terrible news: his father-in-law has cancer. Rachel, Zeke's wife, is so disturbed by the diagnosis that she won't leave her bedroom. Ten years ago, Rachel's mother died of cancer. Since then, the mere whisper of that sinister disease stirs her darkest fears. Rachel's anxious dread seems justified by this latest report from her dad, and now she seems utterly inconsolable.

Zeke knows that Rachel needs him, and he's drawing near to comfort her. He took a few days off work to help out with housework and the kids after the couple got the initial report about Rachel's dad. Zeke has even canceled weekend plans so that they can travel to spend time with her father. But beneath the surface he feels resentment. Zeke would rather be on those weekend outings with the guys. And between his heavy work responsibilities and some commitments at church, he's beginning to feel his energy for giving to others running low. At the end of each day, Zeke feels like he needs someone to minister to *him*. He's starting to feel like he can't supply comfort because he needs so much of it himself.

How does God take people who feel a desperate and preoccupying need for comfort and make them want to keep on providing it for others? In 2 Corinthians 1:3–4, Paul provides three paths to lasting comfort:

- **The Upward Path.** Paul first points the Corinthians up to "the God and Father of our Lord Jesus Christ, the Father of mercies and God of all comfort" (v. 3). This is not Paul including the obligatory spiritual nod so that he can move on to the really practical advice. No, Paul here unveils the cornerstone of all enduring comfort— God himself.

When floods of distress and anxiety overwhelm us, moving upward may not seem very comforting. There's a reflexive human instinct to first reach outward when our souls are weighed down. You've felt it. We want flesh-and-blood comfort. We want to talk it through, find a sounding board, bare our heart, find someone, anyone, with whom we can share our burden. Paul doesn't deny this need, but he does challenge our priorities. For comfort to be ultimately meaningful and durable, it first must spring from an eternal source, "the Father of mercies and God of all comfort."

- **The Inward Path.** What is God's aim when he pours out comfort? Paul tells us that he is the God "who comforts us in all our affliction." Like a top-rated insurance policy, God promises comprehensive comfort coverage. But unlike even the best umbrella coverage, God always pays out. He never fails to deliver on his promises. When the physician calls with terrible test results, God is there. When the job evaporates, he's still there. When the stock market tanks . . . When the teenager rebels . . . When the marriage crumbles . . . Hour after hour, day after day, tear after tear, the God of mercies stands poised to supply us all the comfort we need in the place we need it most—our heart.

God's comforting grace is vast and sufficient to console us in every dark place. Each time afflictions and trials bring temptation, God graciously exposes our cravings for self-pity, self-indulgence, self-flagellation, and self-atonement. And through the many and precious promises in his Word, he shows us how he is better than the false comforts that always let us down.

- **The Outward Path.** Paul presses the point one step further. He gives us the purpose of our being comforted. It's "so that we may be able to comfort those who are in any affliction." Paul tells us that one reason his affliction was given is so that he could first experience God's comfort and then in turn supply comfort and compassion to others.

God is serious about his people helping one another. When he provides comfort for you in the midst of your afflictions, that comfort isn't intended for you alone. God wants you to share the comfort you've received with others when they suffer.

I don't want you to suffer. But I can't begin to describe the difference it makes when someone who is caring for me has experienced suffering and can now sit across the table and understand my cares and calamities on an experiential level. You know it immediately when they speak. There's nothing clinical or abstract; it's raw, real, and relevant. It's also a great comfort to know they are enduring and maybe even prospering. It's a great mercy to see that they've encountered grace. And it's a great relief to know that I'm not going crazy!

If we want our comfort to truly bear fruit, it must be conveyed to others. It must be shared in our churches, small groups, and communities. We have been given a genuine comfort grounded in the God of all comfort. We have something real to offer others. Something that lasts.

Father, when I experience your comfort, help me to see that it's not just for me alone. It's also for others.

DAY

15

When a Spouse Suffers

Isaiah 61:1–11

To grant to those who mourn in Zion—
  to give them a beautiful headdress instead
    of ashes,
the oil of gladness instead of mourning,
  the garment of praise instead of a faint
    spirit;
that they may be called oaks of
  righteousness,
  the planting of the LORD, that he may be
    glorified.

Isaiah 61:3

If your spouse is suffering, they may feel alone. Sometimes there's a temptation to believe no one can understand how they feel or what they are experiencing. Conversely, the person who wants to help their spouse often assumes they know exactly what their mate is feeling. In those moments the words of James 1:19 will help you get traction: "Be quick to hear, slow to speak, slow to anger."

Job's three friends nailed it—until they opened their mouths. They deserve a standing ovation for the first act of their performance. They showed up, sat down, and said nothing: "They sat with him on the ground seven days and seven nights, and no one spoke a word to him, for they saw that his suffering was very great" (Job 2:13). God understands the importance of listening. He always stands ready to listen to us (Phil. 4:6). Show up, sit down, and listen well. The point in this moment is not the poetry of your words; it's your presence.

Then, once the talking starts, ask some questions and listen to the answers. Sufferers don't often understand their circumstances, so they need to know you've heard their heart. Stepping in with questions enhances clarity and stokes your empathy. You might ask, How are you feeling? (Very basic, right?) What helps to alleviate your pain or suffering right now? How is your soul? How can I pray for you? Does this affliction tempt you in any way? Where is God alive to you right now? Are there any lies the enemy is whispering to you in the fire of this trial?

Suffering is a window into the soul. Listening well helps you peer through the window to discover where pain is felt and faith is under attack. It positions you to help—to tell your spouse what you see in their suffering. Even what you see beyond their suffering.

I love this story from Richard Selzer that's included in Alice Gray's collection *Stories for the Heart*. It illustrates just the right balance of silence, listening, and loving care:

I stand by the bed where a young woman lies, her face post-operative, her mouth twisted in palsy; clownish. A tiny twig of the facial nerve, the one to the muscles of her mouth, has been severed. She will be thus from now on. The surgeon had followed with religious fervor the curve of her flesh; I promise you that. Nevertheless, to remove the tumor from her cheek, I had cut the little nerve. Her young husband is in the room. He stands on the opposite side of the bed, and together they seem to dwell in the evening lamplight, isolated from me, private. *Who are they*, I ask myself, *he and this wry-mouth I have made, who gaze at and touch each other so generously, greedily?*

"Will my mouth always be like this?" she asks.

"Yes," I say, "it will be. It is because the nerve was cut."

She nods and is silent. But the young man smiles. "I like it," he says. "It is kind of cute."

All at once I know who he is. I understand, and I lower my gaze. One is not bold in an encounter with a god. Unmindful, he bends to kiss her crooked mouth, and I am so close I can see how he twists his own lips to accommodate her, to show her that their kiss still works.[1]

The husband listened to his wife and heard the fear behind her question. But where the surgeon saw a twisted, clownish palsy, the husband saw something beautiful. When he moved to kiss her, this husband twisted his lips to accommodate her. And in a dark moment where a marriage was tested by suffering, the kiss still worked.

1. Richard Selzer, "The Kiss," in *Stories for the Heart*, compiled by Alice Gray (Portland, OR: Multnomah, 1996), 53.

Love—the kind of love with which we have been loved by the Savior—meets us in our brokenness and sees beauty there. It doesn't try to explain the suffering or assign blame. It simply expresses loving comfort and grateful delight. It shows up. It listens. It cares. It bends to kiss a crooked mouth.

How have you shown delight in your spouse in the midst of their brokenness and pain?

The Moment of Failure

2 Samuel 12:1–15

> David said to Nathan, "I have sinned against
> the LORD." And Nathan said to David, "The
> LORD also has put away your sin; you shall not
> die."
>
> 2 Samuel 12:13

Is there any failure that is following you today? Any botched attempts that visited you shortly after you woke up this morning? All failure lands hard. But there's an exceptional type of failure, the kind that warrants public rebuke. It's the kind that exposes one's worst moments and secret sins for all to see. In such moments of spectacular failure, a person's future plans are instantaneously rerouted through dark alleys filled with devilish snares. Such failure is a surreal tragedy akin to watching your life spontaneously combust like a fireworks finale gone wrong.

It's Joseph exposing his brothers' sins of attempted murder, slave trafficking, and daddy deception when he says, "I am your brother, Joseph, whom you sold into Egypt" (Gen. 45:4). It's Nathan outing David for his sins of adultery and murder with the words "You are the man!" (2 Sam. 12:7). It's Peter saying not once, not twice, but three times, "Guys, read my lips. I *really* don't know him!" (my paraphrase of Luke 22:60).

Recently, I heard about a guy who committed suicide after his involvement in an extramarital affair was made public. No judgment here from me. Only billows of sadness. Who can fully comprehend a despair so great that ending one's life seems rational? But that's one danger when we make a spectacle of failure. The tragedy can foment a shame so great that it overshadows the light of hope and colors the world with night. It's a damp, desperate darkness, a disgrace so damning that it collapses all hope.

Maybe you're there. Or perhaps you know someone who just arrived there. This terrain is so dangerous that only the gospel can survive. Let it speak, and listen well.

First, there's the ugly news. Something wrong has happened by your own hand. You are culpable. So stare at it and don't break the gaze. But also know that, if you follow Christ, you have a reset button called repentance. Confess your sin right now before God and before those you've offended. Own it fully. Your circumstances won't change but your heart will, and that's infinitely better.

Remember, the bloody death and resurrection of Christ breaks into our calamities with the news that this failure need not enslave us. Even for faith-deniers, adulterers, murderers, and enslavers, there is a better word spoken at Calvary. It speaks louder and more definitively than the words of condemnation that swell within.

Now crank up the gospel volume. Turn it up to eleven! That's right, spin the good news dial as high as it will go and let the tune of God's grace drown out the accusations of the evil one. If you can't find the setting, let me provide a jump start:

- Failure attacks identity and seeks to rename you. But your mistakes cannot name you. God has already claimed you; he calls you his child (Gal. 4:7).

- Your failure is not the final word spoken over your life or your future. As long as you draw breath there is more to God's story. And even at death, glory awaits (John 21:15–19).

- People talk and gossip hurts (Prov. 10:18), but the cross reminds us that only a small portion of our mistakes and sins are ever really seen by others. Our sin was so bad that it required God's blood to solve the problem (Heb. 9:11–14).

- Take captive each of the random thoughts that accuse you and replace them with thoughts of God's love (2 Cor. 10:5; Phil. 4:8; Col. 3:2). The judgments of others are a trial only for this life. God knows you fully (Ps. 139:1–4), and still he evaluates you with love and grace in light of Christ's success on the cross (Col. 1:19–20).

- Self-pity seeks to bury us in our failure, but the gospel reminds us that even when life delivers a demoralizing blow, we have been treated far better than our sins deserve (Ps. 103:10).

- The gospel never asks, "What if?" but always, "What now?" Asking "What if?" shrinks the soul under the withering heat of speculation. Asking "What now?" fixes our gaze on the reality of a sovereign God who superintends all things for our good (Rom. 8:28). It asks, "What can I do now to please my good God?" (Col. 1:10; Heb. 13:16).

- Jesus loves you, and because he rose from the dead, he's praying for you (Heb. 7:25).

- This is not your real home (2 Pet. 3:13). Once you arrive safely in the new heaven and new earth, you will see your failure through the eyes of eternity, and you will stand amazed at how God used it for his glory (Isa. 65:17; Rev. 2:1–7).

This good news is God's wisdom for our failures. God reminds us that no matter how spectacular our failures may be, they're never big enough to chill his love or stop his plans. Because of the gospel, there is always hope, always rescue, and always another chance.

In the midst of my greatest failure, Lord, help me to remember your love. You have put away my sin so that I may live! You remember my failure no more.

When You "Get" Mercy

Luke 6:27–36

> Be merciful, even as your Father is merciful.
>
> Luke 6:36

General George S. Patton famously said, "May God have mercy upon my enemies, because I won't." That may be a great strategy for war, but it's hardly helpful in your relationships. Consider Betsy's story.

One week while John, her husband, was out of town for work, she opened a letter addressed to her. It simply stated that John was having an affair. You can imagine the whirl of emotions that flooded her mind in that moment. Betsy moved through dinner and her evening chores with her young boys and then began to process how she would move forward.

Six weeks prior to the letter, John had met with his pastor for a couple of hours and then come home to tell Betsy that he'd been lying, mostly by omission, for the entirety of their fourteen-year marriage. John hadn't been a Christian for long. He'd prayed to receive Christ just a few years before, and Betsy had seen great change. Like many of us, though, John chose to be in charge of his life, and ultimately he became discontent. At that time Betsy had asked him if he had been unfaithful. John said no but admitted that he had been in inappropriate situations. John shared with her that he had a drinking problem when he was on the road and that he had been living a sort of double life.

Betsy forgave John on the spot, and he was stunned at her merciful response. Betsy told him, "Christ forgave us, so why shouldn't I forgive you." In that moment she was actually relieved by John's confession, because he'd become difficult over the last few years and could be quite harsh with her and the boys. His discontentment had become clear and apparent in their home. She was hopeful that this newly forgiven man would begin to grow in Christ again.

Fast-forward six weeks. On the Thursday night that the letter came, things didn't look quite as hopeful. Betsy called her friend to gain some wisdom. They both agreed that calling her husband wasn't the answer. He'd be home on Saturday evening. That left her with forty-eight hours to figure out how she'd respond.

Betsy picked up a book that a woman from her Sunday school class had recommended to her. The book described how mercy is a unique, marvelous, and exceptional word in Scripture. God's mercy means his kindness, patience, and forgiveness toward us. It is his compassionate willingness to suffer for and with sinners for their ultimate good. Betsy read about Jesus's call to love and be merciful toward enemies in Luke 6:27–36, and she began to see that God doesn't simply call us to discrete, isolated acts of mercy but to something much broader—to a merciful disposition of heart and to lovingkindness. Mercy is the kind of love that moves toward rather than away from enemies.

As Betsy read, her heart, which felt like it had been ripped out, began to soften toward her husband. She prayed and fasted as she waited for him to return. As she prayed, Betsy heard God speaking to her. She later told me, "He spoke to me so clearly and told me that the incredible heartache and pain I was feeling didn't even compare to the pain I caused Christ on the cross."

To complicate things, Betsy got word on Saturday morning that her husband's flight had been delayed. He wouldn't be home until late Saturday evening.

Betsy prayed again and then chose to move toward her husband with a severe mercy. She told me, "When my husband came home that night, I greeted him as any loving wife would. God veiled my thoughts of the affair and allowed me to focus on Christ."

In *When Sinners Say "I Do,"* I wrote the following about mercy:

Have you ever wondered where to find the golden rule? It's there in Luke 6:31. As a young Presbyterian, I memorized it like this, "Do unto others as you would have them do unto you." The ESV translates it, "And as you wish that others would do to you, do so to them." Whatever the phrasing, the point is the same. Use how you want to be treated as the measure for how you treat others. Often the golden rule is understood as a way to keep from making enemies. But Jesus gives the golden rule specifically for situations where enemies have already come into the picture. It is his commanded response strategy when we come under attack.[1]

Even though Betsy's husband had become her enemy, she treated him as a friend. She loved him as she would have wanted to be loved herself. She acted with great mercy, and God moved. When Betsy shared the story with me, she and her husband were still together. They still had a long road ahead, but she was choosing to pass along the mercy that she had received from Christ. And that mercy was paving a road of loving perseverance.

How can we act with mercy when we have been the object of serious sin? Or when we know that there may be another sin against us waiting right around the corner? Mercy is not some kind of transaction we make with God where we purchase transformation for our spouse. And it's not appeasing an abusive spouse or sanitizing sinful behavior in the name of God. Our commitment to mercy is an opportunity to show others how God showed his love to us. He extended his mercy before we had changed; "while we were still sinners,

1. Dave Harvey, *When Sinners Say "I Do": Discovering the Power of the Gospel for Marriage* (Wapwallopen, PA: Shepherd Press, 2007), 86.

Christ died for us" (Rom. 5:8). In like manner, we are now called to "Be merciful, even as [our] Father is merciful" (Luke 6:36).

Father, capture my heart with your great mercy, so that, in view of your glory and your mercy shown to me, I might act today with mercy toward my spouse. Amen.

The Moment You Need to Forgive

Matthew 18:21–35; Colossians 3:13

As the Lord has forgiven you, so you also must forgive.

Colossians 3:13

You feel it before you can name it. An old friend mentions someone's name, and a bad feeling washes over you. You see that person at the supermarket, then you taste bile and experience a rush of anxiety. You stiffen when their happy face pops up on social media. When you thought about them today, you had a visceral response. After all, this person hurt you deeply, shamefully, completely, and repeatedly. You were sinned against through betrayal, slander, rage, abuse, or abandonment. Now they smile for pictures while you manage the collateral damage.

The mystery of a broken world is that sinners often move on while the sinned-against are left to clean up the mess. The prophet Jeremiah saw it and felt it:

> Why does the way of the wicked prosper?
>   Why do all who are treacherous thrive?
> You plant them, and they take root;
>   they grow and produce fruit;
> you are near in their mouth
>   and far from their heart. (Jer. 12:1–2)

What are you supposed to do when your spouse has sinned against you in ways that make it hard to move on?

"As the Lord has forgiven you, so you also must forgive" (Col. 3:13). Wow, just think about that verse for a second. The standard of forgiveness we pass along to others must be drawn from how Jesus has forgiven us.

This raises an important question. What did Christ's forgiveness look like?

- *Relationships restored.* Christ does not dwell upon our sins or allow them to pollute the way he views us. He forgave us. He doesn't huddle up with the other members of the Trinity to confidentially gossip about the pain we inflicted on him. When Jesus forgives, the issue dies. It no longer stands between us or obstructs our relationship.

- *Sins forgotten.* Our sins don't remain a point of reference for God. He doesn't keep our transgressions handy for ready reference in case we forget how we've screwed up. Our sins against God are not a card up his sleeve that he plays to check our behavior. Because of Jesus, our sins are forgotten. "As far as the east is from the west, so far does he remove our transgressions from us" (Ps. 103:12).

- *Costs absorbed.* In Matthew 18:21–35, Jesus tells the story of a servant who had been forgiven an enormous debt. But when this servant encountered a fellow servant who owed him a smaller amount, he enforced the penalty for the lesser debt. With this negative example, Jesus teaches us that forgiveness absorbs at least two costs.

First, a spouse must say, "I'm not going to punish you." There's not a person among us who hasn't mentally prosecuted a spouse and delivered the verdict spoken by the unmerciful servant: "Pay what you owe" (Matt. 18:28). For true forgiveness to happen, sometimes a spouse must deny an understandable instinct to throttle their mate and instead release them from punishment, placing their sin under the atoning blood of Jesus.

Second, the one who forgives must literally choose to excuse the debt for their loved one's sin. Just because forgiveness has come doesn't mean the debt has mysteriously evaporated. If I loan you ten dollars and you refuse to pay, the money doesn't magically appear back in my wallet when I forgive you. For Christ to forgive us, he had to absorb the cost of the emotional pain, the shame, and the humiliation of our sins. When we forgive, we say, "I see the cost of forgiveness, and I accept the consequences."

When we forgive someone, we must do what Christ has done for us. We must absorb the cost. I get it; this is hard. It often trips up reconciliation. We want to forgive, but we assume it shouldn't cost us. We instinctively react to the injustice of absorbing a debt. "What? You did it, and now I pick up the tab? Isn't forgiving you enough? Haven't I suffered enough under this situation?" We feel that a sheer willingness not to retaliate is sufficient.

But the cross relieves us of the obligation to enforce punishment for sins committed against us—the smaller debts, to use the parlance of Matthew 18. How can we absorb such injustices? By looking back to the greatest injustice in history, when the spotless Lamb of God was tortured and crucified as a substitute for our sins. We deserved the punishment inflicted on Jesus, but he absorbed the cost. Christ forgave our incomprehensible debt. Now, from the position of being forgiven, we are called to forgive.

You see, forgiveness swings both ways. If we want it from God, we must extend it to others. If we want it, we must share it (Mark 11:25).

Do you remember that person who flashed through your mind when you read the first paragraph of today's devotional? Was it your spouse? An ex-spouse? Someone, perhaps, who has done you much harm? I'm not suggesting you return to an abusive environment or put yourself in a position to be demeaned or taken advantage of. That's a different thing. Right now we're talking about whether you woke up today feeling free of the entrapments of bitterness and resentment. If the answer is no, remember the gospel. "As the Lord has forgiven you, so you also must forgive" (Col. 3:13).

We can't forgive someone we don't pray for. Who did you think about when you read the opening paragraphs of today's devotional? Take a few moments to pray God's best for them.

DAY
19

When You Must Keep On Forgiving

Luke 17:3–4

Pay attention to yourselves! If your brother sins, rebuke him, and if he repents, forgive him, and if he sins against you seven times in the day, and turns to you seven times, saying, "I repent," you must forgive him.

Luke 17:3–4

I t happens in every marriage. The honeymoon spell eventually breaks. You put down the rose-colored glasses, and you begin to look at your spouse more realistically. Sometimes you may become too critical. You see some area of imperfection—in your spouse, of course, not in yourself—and you react with a harsh word or lack of patience.

But then there are times when you experience your spouse's dark side. Something goes sideways in your spouse that is really significant—a way in which they are dulled to their own weakness and sin; a way in which they sin against you profoundly and repeatedly. Maybe they hear God's Word, but something gets lost before it's believed and practiced, like the person who looks in a mirror "and goes away and at once forgets what he was like" (James 1:24). Or maybe they have completely shut their ears to gospel truth (2 Tim. 2:17–18). Regardless, their choices become your burden to bear.

How do you keep your heart tender with love when your words are spent and brokenness still abounds? The answer, of course, is forgiveness.

Jesus says, "If [your brother] sins against you seven times in the day, and turns to you seven times, saying, 'I repent,' you must forgive him" (Luke 17:4). Confessing seven times a day hardly even seems like repentance.

That's just well-managed sinfulness. But it's not our job to parse the souls of others and judge the quality of their confessions. Our responsibility is to maintain a heart that is quick to respond to sincere confessions and anticipates good fruit from the lives of repentant people.

Forgiveness is not only a discipline we practice but also a grace we experience. When we forgive, we lean into the fullness of God's blessing and provision for us: "Be kind to one another, tenderhearted, forgiving one another, as God in Christ forgave you" (Eph. 4:32). Remembering how we've been forgiven strengthens us to wait upon God to convict our spouse of their sin and bring them to full repentance.

In the face of temptation to hold a grudge, we must forgive and then wait. This sort of hopeful waiting supplies power. "But they who wait for the LORD shall renew their strength; they shall mount up with wings like eagles; they shall run and not be weary; they shall walk and not faint" (Isa. 40:31). This is not a setup. God is not playing you, and he's not playing games. By forgiving and waiting, we get lift, we experience resilience, we find strength for the long game. As we sit prayerfully in the waiting room, anticipating the appearance of the Great Physician, a strange thing happens. Faith becomes durable. We may not gain an iota of understanding about why the one we love has chosen this perplexing path. But we have something more valuable than inside information. We know the One who loves this misguided soul far more than we do (John 3:16). He loves to seek and save the lost (Luke 19:10). He promises to reach into our worried days of waiting, kick-start our strength, and help us to persevere in love.

You see, something deeply personal and transformational happens when we endure in forgiving. Our busy heart settles as we expectantly and eagerly pray for repentance and reconciliation in others. We remember that we were once just like them—broken, rebellious, and running away. As we lean into God, remembering how he loved us when we were his enemies, our hearts shift toward the prodigal. Then God works compassion in us so we're ready to receive their repentance when it comes.

And so we forgive and wait. Actively and expectantly leaning toward God, we beat back worry and fear. Applying the gospel, we trust that God's change will come in his time.

God, help me to forgive whenever necessary in a way that displays your patience with me. Help me to do it again and again. Amen.

The Marvin Gaye Moment

1 Corinthians 7:1–7

> Let your fountain be blessed
> and rejoice in the wife of your youth. . . .
> be intoxicated always in her love.
>
> Proverbs 5:18–19

Marriage is more than sex. But as perks go, sex is pretty sweet. In 1 Corinthians 7:1–7, Paul gives the Corinthians a sex talk: "The husband should give to his wife her conjugal rights, and likewise the wife to her husband." Don't get hung up on that word "conjugal." That's not some bizarre Corinthian sexual reference; it simply means marital or wedded. Paul's point is that sex should be a regular part of a Christian marriage, with each spouse consistently supplying their body to the other. That brings me to the subject of Marvin Gaye.

I grew up in the sixties and seventies, when one of my top-ten, all-time most favorite songs was "Let's Get It On" by Marvin Gaye:

> I've been really tryin', baby
> Tryin' to hold back this feeling for so long . . .

Most people wouldn't connect Marvin Gaye with suburban Pittsburgh, but the first time this white kid from the burbs heard "Let's Get It On," it wrecked me. I was utterly transported. From then on, every moment in my parents' car involved a skirmish with my mom for control of the AM radio dial. She didn't get it—I needed my soul fix from Marvin. But Mom totally got it, because this song is entirely about sex. Now, I'm not justifying any unrighteous implications or applications of the song. Marvin Gaye was probably just another voice who moved sex to the center, but his tune soared with soul, and I loved it!

Sometime in the mid-seventies, "Let's Get It On" faded from the airwaves. Presumably it was in a vault somewhere, resting in peace alongside other national treasures like the Federalist Papers and old episodes of *I Love Lucy*.

Twelve years passed. My teenage encounters with "Let's Get It On" were nothing more than faded memories of groovier times. Then one evening, while having dinner with a mission team, I heard the distinctive summons of those first few notes. As a guy who had not heard from Marvin for years, I was delighted at this reunion.

I excused myself to search for the source of the song. Ducking beneath the counter, I strolled back into the kitchen. The area was purportedly off-limits to non-staff, but I had an airtight alibi—Marvin was calling! I walked through the kitchen and down a long hallway to the final door on the right. It was a small storage room.

Sure enough, sitting on a storage rack was a transistor radio with "Let's Get It On" pulsating at full volume from one tiny speaker. I stepped partway into the room, stopped, closed my eyes, and gently leaned my head back against the door. To me, that storage room was Carnegie Hall. "I'm aboard, Marvin. Let the soul train ride!" The next three minutes were practically transcendent.

Unbeknownst to me, there was a custodian squeezed into that small storage room, mopping the floor. But my eyes were sealed shut and my ears were tuned to soul, so I never saw him. Thankfully, the gentleman didn't rebuke me. He just stood watching and let Marvin have his say.

When the song finished, I emerged from my trance to discover this man standing two feet away from me. There was a twinkle in his eye. He was marveling over this strange white dude listening to "Let's Get It On" as if it were Mozart. Before I could mutter an explanation, this prophet began to nod his head and said with a wry smile, "It's a righteous song, ain't it, man. A RIGHTEOUS song!"

Truer words were never spoken.

Yes, I get it. "Let's Get It On" may be another artifact from the seventies that reduced the best of life to sex. Even when dressed in the best of soul, it's still an ensemble fitted for the world.

For Paul, sex is for marriage, and marriage is far bigger than sex. Sex can be postponed as a sacrifice to God during a season of prayer. But sex helps serve our faithfulness. It acknowledges the claims that a wife and husband have over each other's body. It motivates us to loyalty and protects us against sinful temptation. It's one of the tools God uses to glue husbands and wives together.

As you think about your spouse today, consider how you are doing at giving the "conjugal rights." If you feel like it's a weakness, consider the timeless truths of 1 Corinthians 7:1–7. Then dig out Marvin Gaye and surprise your spouse with a truly righteous song!

How are you doing at giving your spouse the gift of sex? Maybe you could each finish the following sentence: "One way our intimacy could be improved would be . . ." After sharing, pray together over your responses and ask God to help you enjoy each other even more.

The Moment of Friendship

Proverbs 18:24; John 15:12–15

Greater love has no one than this, that someone lay down his life for his friends.

John 15:13

C. S. Lewis dedicates the fourth chapter of his book *The Four Loves* to the topic of friendship. One of his key theses is that friends walk side by side. "That is why," Lewis writes, "those pathetic people who simply 'want friends' can never make any. The very condition of having Friends is that we should want something else besides Friends."[1]

No friendship can arise, says Lewis, unless there's something for the friendship to be about. You need a common interest, like music, reading, or stamp collecting for true companionship to be kindled. Lewis writes, "The typical expression of opening Friendship would be something like, 'What? You too? I thought I was the only one.'"[2] Until that moment, the individual was alone. But now he's found a fellow traveler, one who walks in the same direction. You can "fight beside him, read with him, argue with him, pray with him."[3]

Lewis argues in the book that being a friend and being a lover are not the same thing. But the best lovers, he says, are first friends. I'd like to take it one step further. For the fire in marriage to last, friendship must be cultivated and fiercely protected.

What are the conditions that must be met for marital friendship to endure?

1. C. S. Lewis, *The Four Loves* (New York: Harcourt, Brace and Company, 1960), 98.
2. Lewis, *The Four Loves*, 96.
3. Lewis, *The Four Loves*, 104.

First, Jesus must be our friend. Jesus himself said, "No longer do I call you servants, for the servant does not know what his master is doing; but I have called you friends" (John 15:15). Jesus calls us his friends, and he wants us to enjoy intimacy with him. "Fellowship with God," says J. I. Packer, "is the source from which fellowship among Christians springs; and fellowship with God is the end to which Christian fellowship is a means."[4]

Some readers may see this point about friendship and fellowship with God as incidental—like I'm obliged to include something spiritual so we can get to what really matters in the friendship between husband and wife. Not so. Part of the reason the dream of enduring friendship detonates is because the desires for friendship are first horizontal, not vertical. "What fascinations from my world or work should we discuss?" But as Lewis wrote, "Friendship, then, like the other natural loves, is unable to save itself. . . . [It must] invoke the divine protection if it hopes to remain sweet."[5]

If you've been married for more than a month, one thing has become self-evident: Marriage is hard. There

4. J. I. Packer, *God's Words: Key Bible Themes You Need to Know* (Downers Grove, IL: InterVarsity, 1981), 193.
5. Lewis, *The Four Loves*, 124.

are finances, in-laws, sexual adjustments, the arrival of kids (or the fact that kids don't arrive), sickness, lost jobs, teenage angst, conflict, aging, and our sinful responses. How can a person possibly navigate such treacherous terrain? Proverbs answers the question: "There is a friend who sticks closer than a brother" (Prov. 18:24). The ultimate friend who sticks, of course, is Jesus. For true friendship to thrive in marriage, there must be the presence of the Greater Friend.

Second, your marital friendship must be your priority. Never in history has the word "friend" been more dumbed down than in our social media age. First co-opted by Facebook, friendship is now reduced to our list of contacts and virtual acquaintances. They are faces as involved in our lives as strangers we pass while flying down the freeway.

I can remember walking down a set of steps at church one day in the dawning years of social media. My eyes fell upon a circle of young people who were BFFs; they'd all grown up together in the church. But rather than exchanging updates on life and love, or even laughing over shared memories or personal oddities, they were all glued to their phones. It was the strangest thing—friends circled up as they'd been for years, except now they were communicating without words. Their bodies were all present, but their communication was virtual. Besties in a brave new world.

Companionship, the kind that develops into oneness, is one of God's major goals for marriage. At the first wedding in history, cleaving and becoming one flesh were identified as the core benefits of matrimony (Gen. 2:24). These benefits become a reality the moment you say "I do." The challenge comes when couples assume these blessings are installed as mature oaks rather than as tender saplings that must be tended and cultivated. One of the casualties of this idea is that friendships never develop from the pre-wedded romantic stage. As Carolyn G. Heilbrun once said, "Marriage has owed too much to romance, too little to friendship."[6] I agree.

This is why developing friendship makes the defining-moment list. Friendship becomes a dream deferred if we don't fight to nurture it and then protect it. "Hope deferred makes the heart sick, but a desire fulfilled is a tree of life" (Prov. 13:12). Prioritizing friendship means your spouse is your first earthly priority. And yes, this

6. Quoted in Julia B. Boken, *Carolyn G. Heilbrun*, United States Authors Series (Woodbridge, CT: Twayne Publishers, 1996), 121.

means the antiquated face-to-face variety where sitting, looking, sharing, and experiencing each other is not replaced by trendy modes of communication. Prioritizing friendship with our spouse also means they aren't becoming slowly displaced by other people with whom we share hobbies or work interests, or whom we just enjoy being around. It's great for husbands and wives to have such people in their life. They add spice, interest, and opportunities to serve. But we must remember, "A man of many companions may come to ruin" (Prov. 18:24). Ruin follows marriages that don't prioritize the right friendships. Your best friend should be the one you sleep with each night.

Lord, help us to cultivate a deeper friendship. Let us experience fresh delight in the things that once captivated us about each other. Help us to pray together, share together, learn together, and laugh together. Amen.

ENDING TOGETHER

22

When Dreams Come True

Philippians 4:10–13

> I have learned in whatever situation I am to be content. I know how to be brought low, and I know how to abound. In any and every circumstance, I have learned the secret of facing plenty and hunger, abundance and need.
>
> Philippians 4:11–12

U nlike most of us, the apostle Paul did not waste time. At least I don't think he did. Just think about it. Paul taught on contentment . . . from prison! Consider that the next time you're tempted to spend your day binge-watching Netflix. And he wrote, "Not that I am speaking of being in need, for I have learned in whatever situation I am to be content."

When we read Paul saying "in whatever situation," we tend to assume he's preparing us for contentment in suffering, scarcity, and discouragement. You know, those times when the blade of reality dices up our dreams and leaves them bleeding in a ditch. But Paul's not only speaking about when dreams die. The words "whatever situation" cover all of human experience. This means Paul could be content in good times as well as bad. He tells us that he knows how to abound; he's learned the secret of contentment even in abundance.

I understand if you're asking, "Is that really a thing?" If your mind works like mine, a spontaneous prayer may spring from your lips: "Lord, dost thou doubt that thy servant can do abundance and plenty? SMITE ME, O Lord, with a perfect marriage, obedient children, and an overstuffed retirement account! I will show thee that plenty, abundance, and thy humble servant are a trinity of friends who should never be severed!"

Have you ever noticed that when we think about fireproofing our marriage for the future, our mind immediately goes to the sufferings we may endure together or the afflictions that may separate us? We rarely think of good times as something for which we must prepare. We pray for our desires to be satisfied. We want happy marriages, increased incomes, secure jobs, and well-maintained homes. We want to abound because we assume it will better insulate our lives from the seductions that destroy marriages.

But Paul had a different idea. He knew people. He understood temptation, and he recognized that there are enticements embedded in times of plenty and abundance that can unravel a relationship even faster than affliction. "The Christian," said Charles Spurgeon, "far oftener disgraces his profession in prosperity than when he is being abased."[1] That's why Paul had *to learn* to be content in the happy times.

Let me speak honestly to you and your spouse. Most couples believe that contentment will arrive once their suffering leaves. They think that if their circumstances would just improve, they could finally live a life marked by satisfaction. But that's not the way desires work in a fallen world. Contentment isn't circumstantial. God doesn't sprinkle contentment into improved situations

1. Charles Spurgeon, "Contentment," sermon delivered March 25, 1860, *Spurgeon's Sermons: New Park Street Pulpit*, vol. 6, no. 320, www .spurgeon.org/resource-library/sermons/contentment#flipbook/.

so that you just need to hold on until the trial lifts. A richer life and contentment don't walk hand in hand.

Think about it. Do you find wealthy couples to be more content than those in middle-class marriages? Do you find people who enjoy abundance to be more satisfied with life than those who live with hardship? No way. Why? Because regardless of plenty or want, contentment must be learned. And it's *particularly* necessary for the good times.

So, how do we learn the secret of being content?

First, know that contentment must begin today. It shouldn't wait for our spouse to improve, our marriage to feel more stable, the kids to have their breakthrough, the job to get better, or the bank account to be full. Contentment is about satisfaction and peace in the moment, whether the times are good or bad.

Second, know that contentment means looking to Christ. Paul ends this section of his letter with, "I can do all things through him who strengthens me" (Phil. 4:13). He reminds us that true contentment flows directly from Christ. The gospel provides us a daily reminder of what our sins deserved. Though we were spiritually wretched, utterly lost, and absolutely incapable of helping ourselves, God came to us in the person of Jesus Christ. Jesus wrenched us free from our crazed commitment to our own destruction. By dying as our substitute, he gave us hope for this life and beyond. We can now live a life that flourishes on earth not because we have all we want but because we live in Christ, who provides his strength each day.

Finally, no marriage exists where each spouse has everything they desire. But because of Christ's love, we have more than we deserve. And the more we understand this extraordinary truth, the closer we'll get to the secret of contentment in marriage. Whether in plenty or in want, we will never live with all we desire. But we can live with something better—a daily awareness that Jesus has given us enough.

Jesus, grant us peace and contentment until that final day when all of our desires are resolved in you. Amen.

When Conflict Comes

James 4:1–2

What causes quarrels and what causes fights among you? Is it not this, that your passions are at war within you? You desire and do not have, so you murder. You covet and cannot obtain, so you fight and quarrel. You do not have, because you do not ask.

James 4:1–2

I've heard it said that marriage is the process by which love blossoms into vengeance. It's hard to read that without smiling. I think that's because, in spite of the saying's hyperbole, it speaks to a universal reality.

146

Conflict awaits any couple with the courage to say "I do"!

Perhaps you just read that and you're fresh from a painful spat with your spouse. Perhaps conflict has taken up residence within your home like an uninvited squatter. It's always present. Always agitating. Always controlling the course and outcome of any conversation. It visits every night and takes over most conversations. If you're married and live with a lot of conflict, vengeance can seem like the only logical response.

But Scripture says something about conflict that may help you today.

First, conflict doesn't begin outside of us. After James asks the question, "What causes quarrels and what causes fights among you?" he provides a surprising answer. "Is it not this, that your passions are at war within you?" James tells us that the origin of conflict is not in our circumstances, our actions or omissions, or the hurtful things that have been said in the moment.

James gives us a different diagnosis. He tells us that conflict is the result of unsatisfied cravings within our heart. "You desire and do not have." Lurking beneath every conflict is some unfulfilled longing on the hunt for satisfaction. James says, "Your passions are at war within you."

Second, knowing that conflict is stirred by our passions doesn't exclude the possibility that we've been sinned against. When a harsh word comes, it stabs. When our spouse picks a fight, we feel alone and alienated. When we're the object of sinful judgments, we live under the burden of being misunderstood. But experiencing that pain doesn't obligate us to retaliate. Conflict is not a necessary consequence of feeling sinned against.

Let me pose a question for you to think about today. Who was the most sinned-against person who ever lived? It's not a trick question. If you know your Bible, then you understand that Jesus came to earth as the perfect God-man, the spotless Lamb of God. Yet he was rejected and crucified for the sins of those he loved. And those sins for which he died were not just abstract or hypothetical. Christ's road to suffering involved being sinned against personally and repeatedly. Consider the anger poured out toward him, the sinful judgments by the masses, the denial by Peter and the other disciples, and the betrayal by one of his closest friends. The mobs loved him one week and shouted "Crucify!" the next.

He experienced the torture of thirty-nine lashes. He was spat on, mocked, beaten—his beard ripped from his face—and then he died alone and abandoned.

Was there anyone more sinned against than Jesus? Certainly not.

But here's the thing. Jesus did not revile those who mocked and denied him. He submitted to the injustices of Pontius Pilate's kangaroo court without needing to protect his ego or defend his reputation. His heart was pure, which left no room for retaliation. Jesus endured being victimized without demanding vengeance. Jesus suffered without creating conflict.

Now, let me be the first to say that I'm not Jesus. And when I'm sinned against, that fact often shows. When a cutting remark flies in my direction, my first instinct is to return a double portion. In fact, if I happen to be behind a steering wheel at the time, I'll return a hundredfold. But that's not because it's natural and right. It's because I'm fallen. On some twisted heart level, I believe that my own goodness should never be challenged, my name never slighted. I desire and do not have, so I murder with looks and words.

Can you identify with me? If so, there's hope for you.

Finally, James writes, "You do not have, because you do not ask." Hear God's heart for you in these words today. He is your Father. He says to you, "Don't lash out at your spouse when you feel wounded. Instead, come to me. Talk to me. ASK of me!" Take all you feel and the pain you experience to your Papa in heaven. He is poised to listen and then answer your prayers. Jesus reminded us, "What father among you, if his son asks for a fish, will instead of a fish give him a serpent; or if he asks for an egg, will give him a scorpion? If you then, who are evil, know how to give good gifts to your children, how much more will the heavenly Father give the Holy Spirit to those who ask him!" (Luke 11:11–13).

Horizontal acts of retaliation destroy marriages. Vertical acts of prayer transform them. If you're seeking to navigate unresolved conflict today, let me encourage you not to sanitize the activity of your heart. Flee to your Father in heaven. He invites you to come to him. God is not frightened by your conflict-creating desires. He's waiting to commune with you, to forgive you, to guide you. He knows what you need even before you ask him (Matt. 6:8).

Father, when conflict comes, help us reach for you, distrust ourselves, and love each other the way we have been loved by you. Amen.

The Moment of Respect

1 Peter 3:1–6

And let the wife see that she respects her husband.

Ephesians 5:33

S ome passages of Scripture tow considerable freight. God imbues the words with a particular weight of glory; John 3:16 is one of those passages. Others are weighted with our assumptions—the kind of assumptions that can obscure God's wisdom and beauty. Ephesians 5:33 is a verse that's often anchored down in this way: "And let the wife see that she respects her husband."

Husbands come with all sorts of bents and temperaments. Their heart, their gifting, their character, their fruit—all vastly different. This means two husbands may elicit widely different scores on the "respectability scale." Consequently, this passage needs to be better understood for a wife to apply it by faith.

First, the Bible's commands for one spouse aren't intended to reveal the other spouse's God-installed needs. Paul's instruction to "let the wife see that she respects her husband" wasn't inserted in the Bible to enlighten wives to the fact that husbands are all pitiable, insecure souls who *need* respect. Only the most therapeutic of cultures would assume that this exhortation exists to unearth and then satisfy an aching male need.

Second, the passage nowhere says that every husband has earned respect as a right. This is an important point, because Christian husbands often yank the lever of Ephesians 5:33 and expect that their wife's mental machinery should immediately manufacture respect. As a newlywed man, I learned this one the hard way. A wife's respecting her husband is biblical, so I wanted Kimm to respect me. And let me be honest, I defined this in a very concrete way. I wanted Kimm to defer to my decisions, flatter me in front of others, and affirm me in places I felt insecure. I thought being respected in this way was an inalienable right grounded in both Scripture and the US Constitution. It didn't take long before I saw how a good desire can quickly degenerate into a harmful demand. At times I got angry with Kimm because, well, I had an entitled heart armed with a Bible verse.

I genuinely thought this biblical command for my wife (as well as the ones over in 1 Pet. 3:1–6) revealed something to which I was entitled. But over time I came to see that this takes God out of the picture and puts me in his place. Yes, a respectful wife—one who is kind even in disagreement and avoids outing her husband's weaknesses in public—reflects the beauty of God's image and contributes to marital harmony. But God's commands for Kimm exist to help her grow in love with *him* and say something about *him*. They weren't given as a hidden brush to stroke my uncertainties or satisfy my longing to be honored.

Finally, this command calls married women to love their husbands in a way that reflects God's image both to him and to the watching world. When a wife respects her husband, even in the times when he falters or fails, she makes a glorious statement about the power of the gospel in her life. She shows her husband gospel grace when, rather than delivering to her husband what he may deserve, she reproduces Christ's witness in the home. And she can experience joy in displaying respect not because her husband is a paragon of respectability but because she takes joy in pleasing God.

The same principle is in play when the husband is called to "love your [wife] as Christ loved the church" (Eph. 5:25). The force of the command comes not from his wife's loveliness but from Christ's example in loving the church sacrificially. Husbands are called to embody the same costly devotion in the way we love our wives.

Wives, if you woke up this morning next to someone you have difficulty respecting, remind yourself that the motivation to obey this Scripture comes from God and not from your husband's awesomeness. And when you obey God, he is magnified in your home and the truth of the gospel is reinforced. But also remember that your faithful obedience is not meaningless to God. Respectful wives can sow seeds of change. As Peter said, "Likewise, wives, be subject to your own husbands, so that even if some do not obey the word, they may be won without a word by the conduct of their wives, when they see your respectful and pure conduct" (1 Pet. 3:1–2).

An acquaintance of mine recently told a group of people about a woman he knew who trusted that God would honor her obedience. Her husband, to be frank, was a selfish, cynical, and hardened God-hater. While the wife lived with honor toward her husband, he did not treat her with corresponding respect. Over time, though, something happened. Observing his wife's behavior, particularly toward him, tenderized his heart. In a moment of brutal honesty, he saw that his life lacked the character and quality so evident in his wife, and he traced this back to God's activity in her soul.

His wife's respect became a catalyst for his belief. How could she possibly respect such an unrespectable person? It crushed him with conviction and sparked the fire of repentance. God flipped his desires so that he began to live in a way that was consistent with how she'd respected and honored him. Then, as a result of his rapid transformation, the people in his life were amazed by the power of God's work.

Ladies, your war is not against your husband. It's against the weariness that attacks all of us when we don't see immediate change. Stoke your faith. Pray for perseverance. Act in a way that keeps in view the kindness you've received from Christ. And don't grow weary of doing good, for in due season you will reap if you do not give up (Gal. 6:9).

Father, help us to see the kindness and respect with which you have treated us. And help us to transfer the same kindness and respect to our spouse. Amen.

DAY
25

The Moment
of True Leadership

2 Chronicles 20:12; 1 Corinthians 4:2

Moreover, it is required of stewards that they be found faithful.

1 Corinthians 4:2

If I'm going to watch a movie, it's got to have a hero in it. And not a superhero with a cape. I like the guy who is just going along minding his business when circumstances thrust him into some defining role: Bruce Wayne, Jack Bauer, Jason Bourne, or Peter Parker. Just make them a regular guy, understate their training, and throw a life-defining moment at them. Then give me two hours and a tub of popcorn, and I'm good to go.

Husbands, you can probably relate. In our cinematic view of life, the best leader is the unexpected hero, the one who clumsily falls into the role but then somehow saves the planet from annihilation. For a Christian husband, however, there are two fundamental problems with this man-for-the-moment understanding of leadership.

First, most husbands, myself included, don't live in dramatic, one-moment-in-time, do-or-die events—or anything approaching them. Our true leadership moments come in smaller and more frequent doses. They're mundane, obscure, service-driven, and often boring slices of life. When you read exciting accounts of heroic leadership, do you ever wonder, "What did this guy do the next day? Did he take time off? Write thank-you notes? Fix the disposal?"

Any man who walks the aisle and says "I do" quickly realizes that the real work of leadership unfolds in the ordinary responsibilities of life. Yes, big events come, but they don't really define his life. Like a wise sports enthusiast, we must recognize that one victory doesn't guarantee the next. The hardest job when leading is not the big game but the daily grind of getting up and going to practice. On game day, it's showing up and giving your best. First Corinthians 4:2 says, "Moreover, it is required of stewards that they be found faithful." In a world that measures leadership by immediate impact, God calls us to be servants who define success with a longer view—through the rugged beauty of routine, determined, stay-in-the-ring faithfulness. It's the long haul of obedience through consistently loving your wife, patiently leading your kids, working at your job with resolve, and making sure the house is managed that reveals the best leaders.

Second, the call to lead in the home isn't about big events for you. It's about God and your wife. That's the second fundamental problem with a man-for-the-moment understanding of leadership, and it's profound. Often I think my leadership is about showing how great I am. The fact that Dave's call in marriage should be focused on things outside of Dave too easily gets lost. In my mind, what really seems to be needed is more of Dave. But ultimately my leadership is about God's big event, "that Christ died for our sins in accordance with the Scriptures" (1 Cor. 15:3).

Being a great husband plays out in the routine of home life. That doesn't mean, of course, that big leadership moments don't happen. They just won't happen in the way you expect nor will they make you feel like a blockbuster hero. You'll get your leadership moments when you fulfill your pregnant wife's overwhelming craving for cheesesteaks, or maybe chocolate peanut butter swirl ice cream. A true servant-leader will find out a lot about himself when he's asked to change a diaper, clean the kitchen, or give his wife some space when he has *much more* to say. You'll have a leadership moment when you're standing with a troubled teenager who lost a friend and needs words of comfort.

At those times you don't want to be looking for your inner hero. Your secret stash of greatness won't cut it. The servant-leader husband learns to look beyond himself to the God who gives grace and faithfulness in times of need (2 Chron. 20:12). That's the kind of leadership moment you should be expecting. Because in the monotony of real life, where we learn to live from habits of the heart, husbands meet God.

Jesus, help me to believe you when you say that the greatest among us will be a servant. Amen.

DAY
26

When You Want to Care

1 Corinthians 12:21–26

That there may be no division in the body, but that the members may have the same care for one another.

1 Corinthians 12:25

Who helps you when you have a depressing day, a miserable month, or a year worth forgetting? I'm not talking about the people who house-sit or feed the dog for you when your schedule takes you away or unexpected illness hits. I'm talking about something more personal. I want to know who cares for your soul in the dark times. Who knows your temptations and understands the scripts to which you return when you're talking to yourself? Who is asking you where you presently see God working or how his Word is at work in you right now? Who are the people that tenderly probe the substrata of your heart, invite you to reflect upon God's goodness, point you to his promises, and fortify your endurance with a passage or prayer? In other words, who loves you best when you most need care?

In a lasting marriage, the first line of care is most often one's spouse.

I don't want to suggest that your spouse needs to be the only person who cares for your soul. Thank God for pastors, leaders, and trusted friends—not to mention books, podcasts, and other means of grace that lift the soul in timely ways. All of these have been sources of encouragement in my life. But pity the couple that only skate on the surface in their conversations about difficulty and suffering but never plunge beneath the pain and together explore the active workings of the heart.

"Keep your heart with all vigilance," says the Old Testament sage, "for from it flow the springs of life" (Prov. 4:23). That's the responsibility of every believer, but saying "I do" adds a second heart over which we must be vigilant, not with legalistic hyper-accountability but as an expression of genuine love.

What does care look like when it's fueled by love?

Care has feet. We all lead busy lives. With jobs, kids, church, friends, hobbies, and—let's face it—our fixation on the internet, we may be the busiest people in the history of the world. We're always on the move. In this day and age it takes initiative for meaningful care to hit a moving target. Taking initiative gives your love feet. It walks your desire to care directly toward your spouse's need.

If you are going to take initiative and move toward your spouse, you've got to know their burdens. It's pretty simple; you can't help to carry a burden if you don't know it exists. As Proverbs 20:5 says, "The purpose in a man's heart is like deep water, but a man of understanding will draw it out." If you want to know what's swimming in the deep waters of your spouse's heart, you've got to drop the bucket into the well. Don't be intimidated by this step. No one needs a counseling degree to ask helpful questions. Start simply with "How is your soul? Where is the gospel most real to you right now? What have you been thinking about lately? Where are you being tempted?" Questions like these can be asked during evening meals or on car rides when you have only a sliver of time.

Taking initiative also includes praying. Husband and wife, do you pray for each other? If so, are your prayers informed by what you've discovered through plumbing the depths of your spouse's heart?

And don't just pray. Tell your spouse how you're praying for their needs. These conversations are a reminder to your spouse that they are not alone. You're in the deep waters with them, and you're helping them to stay afloat.

Care has teeth. True love has a rugged side. It sometimes says hard things. That's because care with teeth believes that "All Scripture is breathed out by God and profitable for teaching, for reproof, for correction, and for training in righteousness, that the man of God may be complete, equipped for every good work" (2 Tim. 3:16–17). If you truly care, you won't shrink back from speaking words of truth when your spouse indulges foolish or even sinful patterns. You will ask humble questions, but you'll also speak honest truth. A wife, for instance, who knows that her husband, son, or daughter is dabbling in porn, but says nothing, is not loving or caring.

Never forget that the cross is the holy intersection where the perfect love of God met our horrific wickedness. It wasn't God's workaround. He did not ignore our sin or spin it so that our deep transgressions are shown in the best light. No, the sufferings of Christ fully uncovered the scope of our evil. Christ's death shows the world that our sin is so bad that only the Son's blood can take it away. At the cross, the holy God unleashed his wrath against our sin, but not out of spite or hatred. God revealed our sin because of his genuine love for us. "For God so loved the world, that he gave his only Son" (John 3:16). At the cross, we see that God abhors evil, and we see him reveal it in order to accelerate its downfall.

Our own care for our spouse should do the same. Rugged love is genuine enough to abhor what is evil (Rom. 12:9). Biblical care does not manipulate facts nor is it passive toward things that are wrong. Because our care is powered by love, it has teeth.

So let me ask you again: How do you and your spouse care for each other? Does your care have feet and teeth? If not, take some initiative today. Ask questions and be bold enough to speak up when you uncover things that don't align with Scripture. I think you will both discover that even little attempts at soul care can have a big impact.

Lord, help us to care for each other in ways that better reflect your love. Give our care feet and teeth. Amen.

When God Seems Distant

Psalm 139:1–12

> Where shall I go from your Spirit?
> Or where shall I flee from your presence?
>
> Psalm 139:7

We've all had days when God seems far away. Maybe that's where you or your spouse are right now. Perplexed. Doubting. Discouraged. Feeling alone. When God feels distant and the experience lingers, the feeling of distance can extend to other relationships as well, including your marriage. This probably is not a surprise. But knowing this is a common experience doesn't help us get out of that desert place.

How do we help each other in those times when God's presence seems so achingly absent?

Psalm 139 can help. If you haven't read it yet, give it a look-see right now. This psalm is packed tight with truth and remains valid even when our feelings and experiences don't seem to concur. David's words may be a huge help for your marriage today. Let's unpack the passage.

First, God knows you, and it's not in some generic sense. He doesn't know you the way you might know a professional athlete you've read about online. God knows you personally, specifically, and intimately. He knows you in a deep-dive, all-up-in-your-grill sort of way.

How does that hit you? It's both an awesome and awful moment when we discover the One before whom we live fully uncovered. In Rudyard Kipling's book *Puck of Pook's Hill*, the protagonist observes to a friend,

> "Write to any man that all is betrayed," said De Aquila,
> "and even the Pope himself would sleep uneasily. Eh,

Jehan? If one told thee all was betrayed, what wouldst thou do?"

"I would run away," said Jehan. "It might be true."[1]

We can all relate to Jehan. The prospect of having all things revealed makes us want to flee. But that's precisely the scope of God's familiarity with us. God knows when we take a seat and he knows when we stand. He knows when we lie down to sleep and he knows when we get up. God knows everything we're thinking about while we're lying there. And before we speak, God knows what we are going to say. You may not feel very close to God right now, but Psalm 139 makes clear that he's close to you. Even when we feel distance, God is present.

But there's more.

Second, God goes before you. Beginning in verse 7, the psalmist writes about the extreme locations where he'd find God present if he were capable or crazy enough to travel there. If he could ascend to heaven, God would be there. Shoot off to Sheol (that's hell, folks) and God would be there too. If he traveled as

1. Rudyard Kipling, *Puck of Pook's Hill* (1911; repr., Salt Lake City: Project Gutenberg, 2005), ebook, 124.

far as he possibly could or dove down into the deepest recesses of the sea, God would be present to meet him, guide him, and hold him even there.

Even when life's darkness covers you in depression, grief, or despair, God is there providing light. As Psalm 142:3 says, "When my spirit faints within me, you know my way!" Is darkness a part of your story right now? Does it feel like your world has collapsed into a permanent night? Take heart. God is not threatened by a little shade: "the night is bright as the day, for darkness is as light with you" (Ps. 139:12).

Third, God created you. David goes on to unfold another facet of God's comprehensive care. He invites those who feel distant from God to go back to the months before their birth. We don't remember, but God does. He was there working, forming, and knitting us together—making us in a fearful and wonderful way. When they were still secrets to us, God saw our frame and our unformed substance and the moments of each day we'd walk on earth.

You may not feel God's presence today, but he has been intricately involved with every facet of your being since before the days of your birth. His interest in all things you is not to satisfy some craving for juicy tidbits.

God is not the divine paparazzi. He's not a cosmic gossipmonger trawling for your personal information so that he can slander you. No, he loves you with an everlasting love. He looks at you with affection as his created child. God knows your warts and sinful works, but he still loves you.

That's why Jesus Christ came in the flesh. His love and knowledge fueled his pursuit of us. While we were still God's enemies—self-loving narcissists who live in darkness with much to conceal—God sent the Son. Jesus solved the problem of sin and reunited us with our heavenly Father. In spite of his full knowledge of who we are and all we have done, Christ became our substitute. When we were in rebellion, he paid our penalty. Ponder this. Though he fully knew us in our sin, God still fully loved us.

Finally, God invites you. You may feel far from God right now, but because of Jesus, he is close to you. Because he is near, you can ask for his help and anticipate his response. Let Psalm 139 guide you in the requests you make. When God seems distant, you might pray, "Don't forsake me; help me to remember your presence." When you feel blind and aimless, pray, "Jesus, open my eyes, and remind me that you go before me."

When you feel worthless and lifeless, pray, "Spirit, make me alive, and teach me to see how being fearfully and wonderfully made fills my life with value and dignity."

Now try this: Join hands with your spouse and pray the words of Psalm 139:23–24, "Search me, O God, and know my heart! Try me and know my thoughts! And see if there be any grievous way in me, and lead me in the way everlasting!" Amen.

28

When We Discover Words Matter

Proverbs 15:2; James 3:1–10

A word fitly spoken
  is like apples of gold in a setting of silver.

Proverbs 25:11

A great marriage is built through the wonder of words. A lasting marriage comes when two people truly understand the power and impact of speech.

Recently I dabbled in a bit of poetry. That may be a generous exaggeration of what actually happens when I compose a verse. Like most things, I expect I'll learn by doing. But if one is going to experiment with poetry, the wonder of words in marriage seems to be a worthy topic. Here goes.

I love words.

In a broken world, words heal.
Gettysburg is remembered for 272 words.
Words change minds. Mahalia yelled,
"Martin, tell them about the dream!"
Her words found purchase, and fifty years later
    grade schoolers recite Dr. King's words.
Words matter.
By them slaves are emancipated,
citizens united, constitutions crafted,
classics created, civilizations ordered.
Words hail the soul.
Transporting us by music, amusing us by
    rhyme, inspiring us by drama, inciting us by
    eloquence.

In the mouth of a wise man, words sparkle.
When piercing dark minds, words enlighten.
Dark nights, words animate.
Dark times, words illuminate.
From the lips of the prophet, words reform.
On the tongue of a lover, words bond.
When the conscience clefts, words smite.

Two days ago, a confession came from one who
    used words poorly.
He confessed.
I forgave.
A gospel reenactment, courtesy of words.
I *love* words.
I hate words.
Words bite, leaving poisonous marks.
Words wreck, undoing heart and home.
Words obfuscate. "You keep using that word,"
    said Inigo Montoya.
"I do not think it means what you think it
    means."
Words shade meaning.
Words divide,
damage, degrade,
denigrate, disgrace, destroy.
By words Chamberlain placated

and Hitler exterminated.
Words betray, loyal by talk
and deadly by intent.
Small words cause great pain.
Words are fickle.
With many, sin is multiplied.
With few, fools run wild.
With none, evil incubates.
Worshiping words swells the mind;
detesting them damns the soul.
Words mystify, like parables cloaking truth.
Words charm, hissing with temptation.
Words trigger eruptions of anger,
explosions of wrath, declarations of war.
I respect words but never enough.
So I *hate* words.

We need words.
Not the maxims of mortals or the mumblings
    of man.

The Word behind the Prophets, the Psalms,
the Gospels, and the Epistles.
The Word from the beginning.
The Word with God.
The Word made flesh.

The Word who was God.
This Word reverberates,
conveying grace, carrying wisdom,
consoling hearts, capturing imaginations,
cultivating joys, comforting sufferers,
confounding worldliness, correcting sinners,
creating life, communicating the mind of God
to the soul of man.
We *need* the Word of God.
The One spoke words we hated
that we might know the Word who loved.
And because the Word was made incarnate,
upon his Word we stand redeemed.

Lord, help us to live together fully aware of the significance of our words. Even more, help us to turn each other toward your Word and make what you have said the center of our marriage. Amen.

29

When We Want Greater Joy in Our Marriage

Philippians 4:8

Finally, brothers, whatever is true, whatever is honorable, whatever is just, whatever is pure, whatever is lovely, whatever is commendable, if there is any excellence, if there is anything worthy of praise, think about these things.

Philippians 4:8

I f you're anything like me, joy is a reluctant resident within your soul. Occasionally joy slips the bonds of preoccupying responsibility and comes out to play.

The day brightens, the heart lightens, and I see Aslan everywhere. But on most days joy remains a recluse. My weeks are reduced to duty by the absence of delight. For me this is an all-of-life thing. When left to myself, the trenches of my mind have always flowed toward gloomier pools. The fight for joy is uphill and hard-fought.

Yet I have seen progress through determined application of this passage.

My journey toward joy began with seeing the repetition of the word "whatever" within this passage. Whatever! Few words capture our culture of contempt nowadays more than this snappish retort. We hear it often, even among married folks. It's a husband's response to his wife's call about working late. It's a harried mom's exasperated murmur when her husband says he can't pick up the kids. It's a dad's mumble when the kids are AWOL on their chores or a couple's eye-rolling reactions to each other's weaknesses. "Whatever" has become our verbal wave of dismissal. It's the apathy we slip on—sometimes with only a whisper—that shields us from the burden of other people's cluelessness.

But in the Philippians 4:8 fight for joy, God refashions our "whatever" into an invitation. What do we see when we survey our world? Whatever is true, honorable, just, pure, lovely, commendable—it's all out there! Look around you. Do you see the signs?

There is beauty. The sparkling path of a sunbeam, the hue of an autumn leaf, the rippling water of a creek as it cascades across glistening stones. Keep looking. There's much more. Paul said, "Whatever is lovely . . ." When God ordered creation, he stamped "lovely" on everything from the particles within atoms to the planets overhead. It's the dewy grass, the Spanish moss, the stingrays and beach sand, the bumblebees pollinating, and the hummingbirds that hang suspended in midair. Creation reflects God's glory. Can you see the splendor?

There is common grace. God confines sin, upholds natural laws, and distributes gifts and talents. He conveys unmerited blessings upon all people. Can you see grace shining through people outside of your church? How about outside of your faith? A soldier defends his homeland. A wealthy woman supports orphans. An accountant courageously stands against her company's illegal activities. There is virtue, honor, justice, and commendable acts of conscience. It is God's image bursting forth from fallen creatures.

There are worthy things in the world that we should perceive and praise. Paul writes, "Whatever is commendable, if there is any excellence, if there is anything worthy of praise." As you face this day, can you trace the hand of God in what is praiseworthy around you?

And don't forget the worthiest One, Jesus. He's the Alpha and the Omega. He's the captain of our salvation. He is Wonderful Counselor, Redeemer, and eternal Son. He is the Lamb of God who offered himself as a substitute for our sins. Jesus upheld the law of God. Where Adam failed, Jesus displayed perfect obedience. By becoming the second and last Adam, he succeeded where we faltered. By his obedience, Jesus earned for us a super stockpile of righteousness. He imputed it to us through his death and resurrection. This makes him the ultimate "Whatever." He fully and perfectly embodies every quality listed in Philippians 4:8. Our Savior is perfectly true, impeccably honorable, inestimably just, blazingly pure, indescribably lovely, and eternally excellent and commendable.

For people like me who touch joy less often, beholding Jesus helps in the fight for joy.

When was the last time you sat down to calculate and reflect on God's blessings? When was the last time you did it together with your spouse? Think of this as an act of subversion. By returning to each redeemed "whatever" from Philippians 4:8, we stoke a fire in our heart that consumes the bad and animates the good.

Right now, pause long enough to scrutinize your thinking. Where is your mind? What do you tend to dwell on? Which "whatever" grabs most of your attention?

Face it. A fallen mind is always vulnerable to godless thoughts, and to be awake is to be in a constant conversation with yourself. We each have an internal data line from our heart that carries an unending flow of information toward our brain. I'm constantly amazed at how far down the road I can go with unbelieving, God-denying, depressing thoughts before I realize what I'm doing.

But God has not left me without help. In this passage he tells me to move beyond simply perceiving to pondering. God says, "Dave, you're prone to wander. You stray from God-centered, soul-edifying thinking. Let me help you. Think about these things!" Here God guides me in how to fix my mind, and he rescues me from cynical cycles and depressing preoccupations. God says, "Take the good, just, and lovely things you see, and park your mind upon them."

The beauty here lies in the simplicity. It's a step of wisdom so accessible that even a child could manage it without dropping the milk and cookies. Do you see the path? For me, it's made a huge difference. Illuminating thoughts about what is beautiful, grace-filled, and praiseworthy move me more deliberately toward God.

If you can identify with my struggles, let me encourage you. Acquaint yourself with Philippians 4:8. Fight to find that path. Then fight to stay on it! When we ponder the right things, we proceed in the right direction. And along the way we discover something truly remarkable: when "whatever" is redeemed, joy comes out to play.

Lord, we confess that we don't pursue joy. Our minds are scattered and distracted by the things of this world. Help us to think about the glories you point us toward in this passage. Inspire joy in our hearts so we can experience it with greater frequency in our marriage!

When You Look to the Past

Hebrews 13:7

Remember your leaders, those who spoke to you
the word of God. Consider the outcome of their
way of life, and imitate their faith.

Hebrews 13:7

L asting marriages need inspiration. To keep Jesus
first, our marriage central, and our moral clarity
sharp, we must remember courageous believers from
the past who exercised their faith in the face of great
sacrifice. This fallen world is full of people who com-
promise. But the stories of those who stand spark vision
for our own perseverance.

One of my heroes of the faith—a leader eminently worthy of remembering and imitating—is Polycarp.[1] Polycarp led the second-century church in Smyrna, having been appointed to leadership there by men who had seen and heard the Lord. He was widely known for his love of Jesus and his deep convictions about the truth.

When persecution broke out in Smyrna, the Romans rounded up some Christians for interrogation. The persecutors required these believers to renounce Christ and bow before the emperor as a condition of their release. When the Christians refused, they were tortured and executed. Though some bystanders wept with pity for the persecuted Christians, the dramatic spectacle of death in the arena also whet the people's appetite for Christian blood.

Because he was well-known, there was soon a public demand for Polycarp's death. The old bishop didn't flinch or flee. Initially he resolved to remain in Smyrna where the crowds could find him. But Polycarp's companions eventually convinced him to hide at a farm

1. The story of Polycarp is told with greater detail in Charles E. Moore and Timothy Kinderling, eds., *Bearing Witness: Stories of Martyrdom and Costly Discipleship* (New York: Plough, 2016), 8–12.

outside the town. He spent time there in prayer, interceding for members of the church throughout the world.

Meanwhile, in the city the persecution continued. The Roman authorities captured two Christian slaves. One of them broke down under torture and revealed the location of the farm where Polycarp had retreated. When soldiers arrived on horseback to seize him, Polycarp refused to run. Instead, he offered his captors a meal and requested that he be allowed an hour for prayer. When they agreed, Polycarp prayed so earnestly that one hour became two; several of the soldiers regretted their role in the arrest of such a venerable old man.

The soldiers put Polycarp on a donkey and led him back into the city. Upon arrival, his captors ushered him into the carriage of a man named Herod, the captain of the local guard. Herod tried to convince Polycarp to save himself. "Why, what harm is there in saying, 'Caesar is Lord,' and offering incense?" When Polycarp refused the very suggestion, the official grew threatening and forced him out of the carriage so roughly that he injured his shin.

With his escorts, Polycarp marched quickly toward the stadium. He didn't look back. There, a deafening roar rose from the throng of spectators. As he entered the arena, the bishop's Christian companions heard a voice from above say, "Be strong, Polycarp, and play the man."

Polycarp was brought before the proconsul and again was urged to deny his faith and bow before the emperor: "Swear by the spirit of Caesar! Repent, and say, 'Away with the atheists!'" The Romans used the derogatory term "atheists" to refer to the Christians, who denied the existence of the pagan deities. Polycarp saw the irony in the demand. Turning with a grim look toward the crowd that called for his death, Polycarp gestured at them. "Away with the atheists," he said dryly.

Undeterred, the proconsul pressed him further to deny Christ. Polycarp declared, "Eighty-six years I have been his servant, and he has done me no wrong. How can I blaspheme my king who saved me?"

Once more the proconsul urged Polycarp to swear by Caesar. This time Polycarp replied, "Since you pretend not to know who and what I am, hear me declare with boldness: I am a Christian. And if you wish to learn more about Christianity, I will be happy to make an appointment."

Next, the proconsul threatened to burn him alive. To this Polycarp replied, "You threaten me with fire which burns for a little while and is soon extinguished. You do not know the coming fire of judgment and eternal punishment reserved for the ungodly. What are you waiting for? Do what you wish."

At this, the proconsul sent his herald into the arena to announce that Polycarp had confessed to being a Christian. The crowd seethed with uncontrolled fury and called for Polycarp to be burned alive. They gathered wood from workshops and the public baths and assembled a pyre. Then, Polycarp removed his clothes and tried to take off his shoes, though his advanced age made it difficult. His guards prepared to nail him to the stake, but he told them, "Leave me as I am, for the one who gives me strength to endure the fire will also give me strength to remain at the stake unmoved without being secured by nails." They bound his hands behind him. Polycarp offered a psalm of praise and thanksgiving to God, and his captors ignited the wood.

According to onlookers, the flames grew but they did not consume Polycarp. The fire formed a circle around him, but his body did not burn. And since the fire didn't have its intended effect on his body, an executioner was ordered to stab him with a dagger. Observers said that his blood extinguished the flames.

Our lives don't require that much courage—at least not by the standards of this story. But the Bible tells us those days are coming. How do we build a marriage today that prepares for times of testing and persecution? By God's grace we are not left without a witness. We can look back and remember our leaders, those who have lived, loved, sacrificed, and even died to uphold the Savior they treasured. A wise couple will consider the outcome of their way of life and imitate their faith.

Lord, help us not to settle for comfort but to live courageously as a witness to each other, our family, our church, and the community where we live. Amen.

When You Long for Home

John 1:11–14

And the Word became flesh and dwelt among us, and we have seen his glory, glory as of the only Son from the Father, full of grace and truth.

John 1:14

What comes to your mind when you hear the word "home"? Is it a place you inhabit, or is it your family? Perhaps it was the house in which you grew up. Or maybe, just maybe, you feel like Billy Joel, who sang, "I never had a place that I could call my very own; but that's alright my love, 'cause you're my home." Home for you is embodied in a person—your spouse.

Maybe home even evokes the idea of loss.

My uncle Lou died a few years back. His parents immigrated from Italy, and Uncle Lou held a conviction deep down in his DNA that home meant food, wine, and parties. In the early evening, my family would pile into our car and drive to Uncle Lou's house. Other family members from different corners of Pittsburgh would also converge at the appointed time. Uncle Lou's home would swell with people as the family piled in, adults descending to the basement and kids deployed toward the living room. Everyone knew their assigned place. Eventually the adults would reach a level of relaxed detachment and the kids were invited to join them. And if all the stars aligned just right, Uncle Lou would break out his accordion.

Would to God that every person in the world had an Italian uncle who played the accordion! I think our best shot at world peace is to toss our global leaders together in a room for a night with an Italian uncle riffing on that instrument. When the accordion came out at Uncle Lou's, the singing would commence, a few folks might dance, and we children would sit back and marvel that adults could have so much fun.

When I think about home, I sometimes think of accordions and Uncle Lou. How about you? What comes to your mind when you hear the word?

As we arrive at the final day in our devotional journey, I thought about this question and a well-known passage about the incarnation, John 1:11–14. In a strange way, I seem to connect the idea of home with Christ coming to earth. But maybe not in the way you might think. For our Savior, the incarnation didn't mean coming home but leaving home.

When we think about Christmas, it's easy to reduce it to the friendly story of Christ's arrival—the angels, shepherds, manger, and wise men. But before Jesus came to earth, he had a delightful experience of home that he had to leave. The members of the Trinity—Father, Son, and Holy Spirit—eternally coexist in perfect unity and joyful community. The glorious impulse that pervades God's being, the divine quality that courses through each person of the Trinity, is *love*. Think about that. The Son experiences an unending deluge of irrepressible acceptance and unstoppable affection, and it sparks an ecstatic delight in his experience with the Father and the Spirit.

That doesn't sound much like our families, does it? For many of us, family time includes tension, conflict, and skeletons that keep popping out of closets where we wish they'd remain hidden. When families gather in this fallen world, drama abounds. But that's my point. Jesus wasn't running away from any ugly family drama. Before he came to earth, the Son's preexistent experience was only spectacular, unrelenting, and deliciously magnificent love.

Then God became flesh.

Compelled by love, the Son moved out. He "did not consider equality with God something to be used to his own advantage; rather, he made himself nothing by taking the very nature of a servant" (Phil. 2:6–7 NIV). Divinity took on humanity in a union of nature and existence. But Christ's divinity remained cloaked, like a hidden superpower except infinitely more splendid. Out of his boundless love for us, the Son laid aside the glory of his preincarnate experience (John 17:4–5), the treasure of his heavenly home (2 Cor. 8:9), the independent exercise of his will as the Son (John 5:30), the use of certain privileges such as his omniscience (Mark 13:32), and the unbreakable experience of joy-filled communion with his Father (Mark 15:34). The Son's experience of home changed.

But why? John 1:11–12 says, "He came to his own, and his own people did not receive him. But to all who did receive him, who believed in his name, he gave the right to become children of God." Christ came so that we might experience a radical redefinition of family. Jesus came to earth on a mission to make us God's children. This reality gives focus to the wondrous news of the Son's self-emptying sacrifices. You see, *Christ left heaven to bring us home*. The goal of this life is to let him.

Our marriage and family, as wonderful and indescribable as those gifts are, don't ultimately satisfy our deepest longings. Even after the best family event, vacation, or date night, something is missing. It's elusive, a feeling of exile that shadows us each day. We can't always find words for it, but still we long for a place where we can feel fully present, wholly engaged, undistracted by wrong desires, and enraptured by joy. We know this place exists, but we also know that our marriage alone cannot deliver us there.

It's a kind of homesickness, a daily pining for the place we're made for. It's a redemptive reminder that we are absent from the world for which we are best fitted.

We are exiles, wandering lovers, married to each other for a journey that ultimately transports us to another home, the dwelling of our Father and eternal family. The new heaven and new earth await us. We are not home yet!

Today, the day I'm writing this devotional, is the funeral of a dear friend. He left behind a loving wife and three dedicated children. The day will be spent comforting one another with the reminder that he went home to be with the Lord. Yes, he tragically left behind his wife and kids. But Kevin has finally gone home.

My friends, rejoice in the wife or husband of your youth (Prov. 5:18). But do so remembering that the home you build on earth is not permanent. You and your spouse were made for another land. Like my dear friend, you too will one day arrive at home. May God use your home here to prepare you to live in the place for which you were truly created.

Lord, thank you that Christ left heaven to bring us home. Help us to live each day preparing and anticipating together for our permanent home in heaven with the Father. Amen.

Dave Harvey (DMin, Westminster Theological Seminary) serves as the president of Great Commission Collective, a church-planting ministry in the US, Canada, and abroad. Dave founded AmICalled.com, pastored for thirty-three years, serves on the board of CCEF, and travels widely across networks and denominations as a popular conference speaker. He is the author of the bestselling *When Sinners Say "I Do,"* as well as *Am I Called?* and *Rescuing Ambition*, and is a coauthor of *Letting Go: Rugged Love for Wayward Souls*. He and his wife, Kimm, have four kids and four grandchildren and live in southwest Florida. For videos, articles, or to book an event, visit www.revdaveharvey.com.

Connect with
DAVE!

To discover more content from Dave Harvey and
find more resources for marriage and ministry, visit

RevDaveHarvey.com

  @RevDaveHarvey

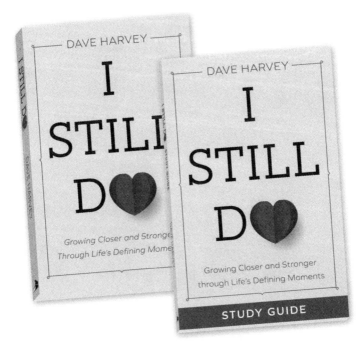

Connect with
BakerBooks
Relevant. Intelligent. Engaging.

Sign up for announcements about
new and upcoming titles at

BakerBooks.com/SignUp

@ReadBakerBooks